PUFFIN BOOKS

THE UFO INVESTIGATOR'S HANDBOOK

'What does all this stuff about flying saucers amount to?
What does it mean? What is the truth?'
– *Winston Churchill*

'I am convinced that these objects do exist and are not
manufactured by any nation on Earth.'
– *Air Chief Marshal Lord Dowding*

'I must insist upon full access to disks recovered ...
The Army grabbed one and would not let us have it ...'
– *J. Edgar Hoover, Director of the FBI*

'I can assure you that there is not a grain of truth in the
allegation that there has been a "cover-up" about alleged UFOs.'
– *Rt Hon. Michael Heseltine MP*

'I am convinced that UFOs exist, because I have seen one.'
– *Jimmy Carter, US President*

'If people only knew how true this really was ...'
– *Ronald Reagan, US President,
to Steven Spielberg at screening of* ET

'We all know that UFOs are real.
All we need to ask is, where do they come from.'
– *Apollo 14 astronaut Edgar Mitchell*

'SPAAAAAACE – MAAAAAN!!'
– *Babylon Zoo*

The UFO
Investigator's Handbook

Marc Gascoigne

PUFFIN BOOKS

PUFFIN BOOKS

Published by the Penguin Group
Penguin Books Ltd, 27 Wrights Lane, London W8 5TZ, England
Penguin Books USA Inc., 375 Hudson Street, New York, New York 10014, USA
Penguin Books Australia Ltd, Ringwood, Victoria, Australia
Penguin Books Canada Ltd, 10 Alcorn Avenue, Toronto, Ontario, Canada M4V 3B2
Penguin Books (NZ) Ltd, 182–190 Wairau Road, Auckland 10, New Zealand

Penguin Books Ltd, Registered Offices: Harmondsworth, Middlesex, England

First published 1996
1 3 5 7 9 10 8 6 4 2

Copyright © Marc Gascoigne, 1996
All rights reserved

All photographs supplied by Fortean Picture Library

The moral right of the author has been asserted

Typeset in Monotype Baskerville

Made and printed in England by Clays Ltd, St Ives plc

Contents

*This book is for Liam and his friends
who were playing with their walkie-talkies in my street that
Saturday morning: 'We've just picked up a UFO – listen!'
And people ask where I get my ideas from . . .*

There's Something Out There

'**A**ttention, Earthlings! Your planet is being invaded!'

Our skies are full of flying saucers: sleek silver discs, sinister black triangles and clusters of tiny drones that circle around vast motherships. On the ground, so-called 'Greys' are snatching people from their beds. Men in Black steal evidence, interrogate and intimidate witnesses.

Rumours are circulating: the American government is working, hand in hand, with the aliens to develop new and secret technologies. Captured aliens are being kept underground in hidden desert bases. And more, much more . . .

There are UFOs everywhere. Or, at least, so some people would have you believe. But what is the truth? This is a question many people are finding it harder and harder to answer.

It's all down to *The X-Files*, of course. No other single event has sparked as much new interest in the subject of UFOs and the paranormal in general. Millions follow the

© Fortean Picture Library

An American military plane saw a dark-red UFO at 4000 metres over Utah, USA, in 1996, and the pilot took this photograph.

adventures of Special Agents Mulder and Scully every week, as they investigate the world of the weird.

Have you ever thought, while you were watching that show, what it would be like to actually *be* a UFO investigator? To be on the look-out for sinister flying saucers and alien abductors, searching for the true explanation for mysterious crop circles and inexplicable happenings? Well, now's your chance, because this book will tell you all you need to know to do just that!

There are vital questions that need to be answered for the sake of all mankind. Are there really alien beings, and are they visiting our planet? No one knows the answer to that one for sure – yet. So slip on that trusty raincoat, grab your notebook and start investigating. The truth is waiting to be found.

How to be a UFO Investigator

So, you want to be an investigator, do you? Well, we're sorry to have to tell you that the FBI doesn't usually sign up people as young as yourself to be an agent in their UFO investigation department. Also, it has to be said, they do prefer them to live in America and be fully qualified secret agents. Sorry about that.

Don't worry, though: it's far easier to be an amateur investigator – for a start, there are no horribly difficult entrance exams. And all those endless reports and other pieces of paperwork which agents have to write seem far too much like homework to be fun. Anyway, you know how it is with senior government officials: they're always losing vital evidence or tearing up your reports on Orders from Above. Believe us, you wouldn't want bureaucrats like that telling you what to do all the time.

No, stay independent. Then your investigations should have a better chance of getting that much nearer to the Real Truth.

Creating your own UFO files

There are two distinct sides to being a UFO investigator. It's great running around seeing UFOs all over the place, being carried up and away by a flying saucer or going for a ride on Nessie's humps – but, let's face it, such events don't happen every day. Most of an agent's time, in fact, is spent assembling data and information, in order to discover the truth of a case.

Every individual case is known as a File, and each one must stay open until a proper, provable explanation has been found for the events described in it. As you can imagine, many of the classic files remain unexplained to this day. But of course *you* weren't on the case back then, were you?

Create your own files on UFO cases, collecting every scrap of information you can find. Include witness statements, photographs, drawings, clippings from newspapers and magazines, and so on. The smallest, most insignificant scrap of evidence may be just the thing to blow a case wide open.

Research is the key

A keen investigator should be familiar with all the latest theories concerning UFOs and their supposed explanations. You already hold the most useful aid to that in your hands (this book, stupid). To help expand your investigations, we have added a section on further reading at the end of this book. There are also several magazines for UFO fanatics. Your local library will be able to help track down obscure titles . . . that is, if the government haven't withdrawn every copy to stop the Truth getting out!

Read as much as you can on the subject, but don't forget to swot up on hoaxes and frauds with just as much care as on apparently real sightings. Many UFO books are written by people who believe absolutely everything; even when hoaxes are exposed, some so-called experts refuse to admit that it wasn't all proof of an alien presence! Also keep an eye out for television news reports and special documentaries on famous cases like Roswell. Some will not treat the subject very seriously, but others may well help you close a file.

These days agents have access to the latest high-tech analytical devices. You do too, if you have a home PC. Keep all your records in computer files – but remember to make copies in case some sinister government agency decides to make off with them as part of a cover-up. Separate the files into categories: not just date, time and place, but type of encounter (see page 9), any similarities to other cases, and any possible explanations. Look for patterns!

The Internet is a vital resource for many UFO investigators. Because it cannot be censored, it is home to all kinds of strange debates and explanations for the UFO phenomena – but the truth must be out there somewhere. Keep tuned in to the UFO home pages on the World Wide Web for the latest developments, and discuss alien issues in the various news-groups. We have provided a handy list of addresses at the end of this book.

FILE STATUS

Various cases in this book are marked with our opinion of their current status. This may be a conclusion, such as solved, hoax — or still open and unexplained. As you continue your own investigations, you may be able to solve some of these for yourself! Watch out for the latest news based on government reports, independent UFO investigations, and the Internet.

Agents in the field

If you are lucky, you may get a chance to investigate an actual UFO sighting for yourself. You must be ready to spring into action at any time. Generally, aliens don't make appointments to be spotted. Be alert!

Luckily, the most important pieces of equipment you will need as an investigator are with you already: your brain and your senses. With them you'll be able to make sightings, and then (hopefully) be able to explain them. Get into the habit of keeping your eyes and ears peeled for anything out of the ordinary. Also, as you will soon discover, many frauds and hoaxsters are lurking around and there are also simple misunderstandings and confusing reports, so investigators will need their wits about them if they are ever to winkle out the truth.

You will need equipment to record any strange sightings or encounters you may have. A dedicated investigator will carry this around with him or her at all times – for you can never tell in advance when something unusual will happen!

A notepad and pens are essential for writing down every last detail, no matter how trivial, and for making sketches and diagrams of what you saw. If you ever do come across something strange, make a note of every last detail. The smallest and most trivial thing could be vitally important in establishing what has occurred. Oh, and make sure your pens work; there's nothing worse than trying to draw that fabulous, 100-metre-long, glowing flying saucer with a chewed-up purple felt-tip or a broken pencil.

Use a watch to record the time of any strange happening – and note how long it goes on for, too. As you'll read later, some peculiar encounters have resulted in watches stopping or skipping a few hours. As yet there's not much you can do about that: no one seems to sell UFO-proof watches yet. (We asked in a number of shops, but they just kept asking us to leave – could this be more evidence of a government cover-up?)

High-tech help

A camera will come in extra handy for proving whether you did or didn't see something peculiar. If you do carry a camera, you should know how to use it. You'll need the right film for the time of day and weather; taking pictures at night is particularly tricky, worse luck. If you have a telephoto lens, even better. Practise whipping out your camera and snapping off a shot that's properly in focus. More importantly, perhaps, you should be able to take a photo without sticking your stupid great thumb over the lens. Also practise taking off the lens cap.

If you ever find that you have snapped something peculiar, make plenty of copies. Keep the original negatives safe, and never ever give them over to strange men dressed in black who claim to be from the government . . .

If you're lucky, you may have access to a video camcorder. These are even more useful, as they can take many more shots than a regular camera, and they can also prove that an object is moving. However, they are far more complicated to control and focus, and their picture-quality isn't always as good as still film.

If you're *skywatching* (that is, sitting around scanning the night-sky for anything unusual) a telescope or binoculars will be very handy. Other useful devices can include a small tape-recorder for picking up odd sounds and for you to dictate your experiences into; walkie-talkies may help you keep in touch with your fellow investigators. Some experts recommend carrying a thermometer, so any changes of temperature can be detected and analysed – though a keen investigator like yourself will surely notice if it suddenly gets very cold or very hot. Finally, some tasty snacks and a flask of something to drink will help those long skywatches pass more quickly.

The Golden Rules of investigation

Look for the truth: Almost everything that people see in the sky, or encounter on the ground, can be explained as a perfectly normal occurrence. It is so easy to go out looking for UFOs and then see them – precisely because that's what you want to see. What UFO investigators are looking for are those very rare encounters which cannot be explained by rational means; and, beyond those, that one golden event which will actually prove the existence of alien visitors to our planet. Be patient; the truth is waiting to be found.

Beware of hoaxes: People love playing tricks (particularly on gullible UFO fanatics), so watch out for hoaxes and fakes. Just as importantly, *don't ever* be tempted to carry out a hoax yourself. It may start out as a harmless bit of fun, but matters often get out of hand. Whether it's sticking a few UFO-shaped pieces of card on your window and then taking a photo, or making a crop circle in the shape of Sonic the Hedgehog with your mates, just DON'T DO IT.

Be safe: Always tell an adult where you are going; better yet, rope one in to assist in your investigations. Get permission if, say, you want to sit in the garden skywatching late at night. Follow all the usual rules about not talking to strangers. UFO investigating is supposed to be fun, but don't be dim; stay safe.

Rating the unusual

To try to make it easy to start explaining unusual sightings, a framework has been invented in which every event can be placed. If you've ever seen the movie *Close Encounters of the Third Kind* you'll have come across part of it already. It was devised by UFO expert Dr J. Allen Hynek of the Center for UFO Studies in the early 1970s, and has since been expanded to cover other types of encounter.

Throughout this book we will be examining the different types of encounter, with classic case-histories and (hopefully) some explanations. That said, however, don't assume that each of the 'Close Encounter' ratings mark out a specific time, a new development in the UFO explosion. It's not the case that, say, First Kind encounters happened in the 1950s, Second Kind in the 1960s and so on; in fact, the first modern CE2K (Close Encounter of the 2nd Kind) happened only a week after the first CE1K! Most UFO encounters are still plain First Kind sightings, and abductions and beyond are very rare indeed – if they happen at all.

Distant encounters

First of all, there are three types of distant encounter, usually regarded as occurring at least 150–200 metres or so from the viewer. You'll have to guess these distances; most UFOs don't stick around long enough for you to get to them with a tape measure.

Daylight Discs (DD): Sightings made during the daytime. These are usually of 'flying saucers', disc-shaped craft hovering or moving at great speed. Sometimes they are metallic or black, occasionally little more than a bright light.

Nocturnal Lights (NL): The largest category of UFO sightings, these are unexplained lights seen in the night sky. They may be any number of colours, and may stand still or move about. There may be one or several of them.

Radar-Visual (RV): You are unlikely to come across these yourself, as this category is specifically for those strange blips that turn up on the radar screens of air-traffic controllers, whether working at a civilian airport or for the military. They are sometimes seen at the same time as reports of the other two types.

Close encounters

If an encounter takes place *within* 150–200 metres, it then falls into one the following 'Close Encounter' ratings:

Close Encounters of the First Kind (CE1K): Seeing a UFO of some sort, whether in the sky or on the ground. No contact is made and no physical evidence is left behind. Almost all UFO sightings are of this sort, and most of them are easily explained as being something other than an alien spacecraft.

Close Encounters of the Second Kind (CE2K): The UFO interacts with the viewer or environment in some way: it leaves dents or burns on the ground or, more seriously, it stops watches, turns off a car's engine or injures the viewer. If a UFO lands in your garden and flattens faithful Shep's kennel, that's a CE2K.

Close Encounters of the Third Kind (CE3K): A sighting of the occupants of a strange craft, but usually without any specific meeting or interaction with them. In other words, you can wave, but they mustn't wave back if they want to qualify as a CE3K.

Close Encounters of the Fourth Kind (CE4K): Added more recently, this means that the witness has met the occupants of a UFO or has even been taken on board their craft. This has come to mean abduction by aliens!

Although it has not been universally agreed on, some experts are now talking about a Fifth Kind: *Direct Communication.* That is, encounters deliberately made between the government and scientists and the aliens, chiefly, it seems, to acquire futuristic alien technology.

Sounds far-fetched? We'll see.

UFOs in History

Mankind has been seeing weird objects in the sky ever since the dawn of time. In Ancient Times, of course, anything huge and shiny, like the Sun and the Moon, was worshipped as a god. These days, our skies are packed with jet planes, helicopters and hot-air balloons, and our planet is orbited by literally hundreds of satellites.

There have always been sightings and encounters

which cannot be explained by rational means – and it's these that you will be investigating. Before you can start, you need to know something about how modern *ufology* (the study of UFOs) came to be what it is today, by analysing some cases from way back in history.

Ezekiel's vision

Many studies of UFOs in history begin with a strange Bible story. The Book of Ezekiel tells the story of that prophet's peculiar vision: he saw a strange vehicle which descended from the sky, firing bolts of lightning! After it landed in the desert in a whirlwind of sand, strange, four-winged and four-headed beings emerged from the vehicle! Bible scholars tend to interpret the vision as a dream or a symbol, but some ufologists treat it as if it were a true story.

Similarly fantastic encounters are reported in other ancient texts. For example, in 329 B.C., Alexander the Great's army was said to have been attacked by flying 'silver shields' that came down from the sky. The Roman writer Livy described a bizarre 'flying altar' that soared high above the Italian countryside in 214 B.C.

In the Middle Ages, too, if you believe the writings of some scholars of the time, the air was full of odd creatures and alien devices, from dragons to giant floating eyes. In 1561, the sky over Nuremberg in Germany was said to have been filled with 'cylindrical shapes from which emerged black, red, orange and blue-white spheres that dart about' in 'a very frightful spectacle'. Just a few years later, in 1566, Basle in Switzerland suffered a similar scare; a scholar called Samuel Coccius wrote at the time that 'many large, black globes' filled the sky, zooming about at high speed for many hours!

After all this time, it's hard to determine the truth of such reports, let alone start looking for an explanation for them. There is no firm evidence to prove or disprove that these were alien phenomena – not that this stops some UFO investigators from seizing on them as evidence of ancient alien invasions!

Built by aliens?

Investigators sometimes point to the world's greatest ancient monuments, from the Great Pyramid and Stonehenge to the strange statues of heads on Easter Island. Because they are so huge and well made, primitive people couldn't have made them without help, they argue. Who helped? Why, aliens of course! As archaeologists discover more evidence that humans were, in fact, perfectly capable of moving rock slabs on wooden rollers, or of carving and raising the Easter Island heads, these theories are being disproved.

True, there are some ancient constructions that so far have defeated explanation. The strange markings in the desert at Nazca in Peru are a case in point. Here, far from any settlement, the desert floor is covered with immense drawings of animals, flowers and symbols picked out in indentations and lines of stones. They were made over the course of several hundred years, starting around 2000 years ago. They are all but invisible from the ground – but from the air they are spectacular!

Strange markings in the desert at Nazca, Peru.

This has led to various 'experts' announcing that they were *obviously* runways for alien spacecraft. Why would spacecraft need runways in the shape of a spider or a fish? Besides, the ground is far too soft for anything to land on. More recently, scholars have tried to prove that the ancient people here flew primitive balloons, but for now the reason for the ancient lines at Nazca remains unexplained.

The Great (American) Airship Scare

The first, proper, controlled airship flight was made in France, in 1903, only a few months before the Wright Brothers made their epic aeroplane flight. For more than a decade after that, airships were both very rare and unreliable. But there is a long series of reports of strange airships and other craft seen in the skies above Europe and the United States from the 1880s onwards!

A huge, cigar-shaped craft, driven by a mighty propeller, was seen shining searchlights down over Sacramento, California, in November 1896 – by more than 200 witnesses. Their stories were carried by local newspapers across the country. A genuine wave (a long series of UFO sightings) started, with peculiar vehicles being spotted over Texas, Canada, the Midwest and the Great Lakes until May 1897.

Interestingly, in 1886, the great French science-fiction writer, Jules Verne, author of *Around the World in 80 Days*, had published his novel *The Clipper of the Clouds*, in which a terrifying craft is spotted hovering in the sky around the world. It encouraged many other writers to produce similar adventures based around sinister flying machines. Could it be that such books influenced what people thought they saw in the skies?

Certainly some people were being inspired by the scare to invent their own sightings. In April 1897, a 100-metre-long airship was alleged by Texan cattle-rancher Alexander Hamilton to have sailed down out of the sky, lassoed a cow and flown off! The story was widely reported, but it was a hoax – albeit one that is being reported as true even today! In Dallas that same month, the *Morning News* printed a story about a mysterious airship that had crashed in the town of Aurora. It was said that the body of a flyer had been found and declared by an astronomer to be that of a dead Martian! It wasn't until 1966, when UFO researchers looked into the story more closely, that it was found to have been a hoax thought up by a telegraph operator who had sent the story in. Make a note: as long as there have been sightings, there have been hoaxes!

> **FILE STATUS**
> It all happened too long ago to know for sure.
> Some definite hoaxes.

The Great (British) Airship Scare

Strange airships continued to be reported from time to time all over the world, from Sweden to Australia. In 1909, another truly major flap started – this time in Britain. In March, P.C. Kettle, a policeman patrolling in Peterborough, heard the sound of a car approaching. He was startled when the sound moved above him – and he looked up to see a bright light attached to a long, dark, oblong-shaped craft gliding over him and moving away over the horizon!

The next sighting was made at the beginning of May in Northamptonshire; but it was in Cardiff, a few days later, that the most important sightings were made. A couple of dock workers spotted a sinister, oblong-shaped craft, and it came out that the previous night more than a dozen witnesses had seen the same craft over the other side of the city. It was 'long and like a big cigar', said a Mr C. Lethbridge, who even claimed to have seen two men in odd uniforms jump into the airship and fly off!

The very next day the *East Anglian Daily Times* threw a wider angle on the incident, with the dramatic headline **'BRITAIN INVADED! AIRSHIPS IN EAST ANGLIA, WALES AND MIDLANDS!'** Sightings of the dark airship were reported from as far afield as Birmingham, London, Norwich and Pontypool!

With so many sightings being made, all kinds of explanations were offered by 'experts' to try to clear up the matter. The planet Venus was a popular explanation offered by many (and it continues to be to the present day, as we shall see), but a bright light near the horizon is plainly very different from a moving, black cigar-shape. Many people were convinced that the Germans were responsible, since they were preparing for war. However, German Zeppelins were still very unreliable, and in fact the German army had only two such airships at the time – which could hardly account for the many sightings over such a wide area.

No real explanation has ever been found, and the stories are now lost in the confusions of the past. However, the way the scares developed is very revealing; many of the UFO flaps that happen today do so in a very similar way.

> **FILE STATUS**
> Unexplained; it all happened too long ago to discover the truth now.

Foo fighters

Yes, we know, you're thinking 'How does a top grunge band fit into the history of UFOs?' Well, Dave Grohl's group are named after a phenomenon which has been affecting pilots ever since it was first reported during the Second World War.

Allied pilots flying night raids over Germany late in 1944 were startled to find themselves surrounded by small glowing balls of reddish or silver light. These shot up towards the aircraft from the ground, shimmered around their fuselages and along the edges of their wings, and in some cases even caused the planes' engines to misfire. Soon reports were also coming in from pilots fighting in other parts of the world.

Named after a catchphrase from the comic strip *Smokey Stover*, 'where there's foo there's fire', these *foo fighters* became so commonplace that an official investigation was called. At first there were worries that the fireballs were a new German weapon, sent up either to affect the planes' electrics or even to confuse pilots. At the end of the war, it was discovered that enemy pilots had also been startled by the strange lights – and had assumed they were a new American secret weapon!

Suggestions that the balls were a form of static electricity discharge like St Elmo's Fire were soon disproved, for many pilots had already experienced such effects, and these weren't the same. Some said that pilots were merely being confused by distortions caused by ice on their canopies, but this theory was disproved when word came that some German prisoners had seen a low-flying bomber with a ball of light clinging to it. What was certain was that many pilots were witnessing these strange lights, and their unease about them was being passed by word of mouth among the squadrons.

The official investigation into foo fighters was possibly the first proper inquiry into genuine UFOs. After the war ended, it was finally decided by air force experts that the foo fighters were solely the result of, well, 'mass hallucinations': the minds of all the pilots were apparently playing tricks on them!

It was a strange conclusion, given that there are even photographs taken during night-time missions that appear to show glowing balls of light, just as the pilots described. This wouldn't be the last time such a conclusion was drawn by those in the government about what was a genuine and well-witnessed phenomenon . . . Needless to say, despite such assertions, foo fighters continued to be seen by fighter pilots flying missions in Korea and Vietnam and elsewhere.

All these years later, it is very hard for investigators to offer any real explanations for them. Indeed, previous flaps like the great airship scares were all but forgotten, only to be rediscovered by researchers in the last twenty years. In America in 1947, however, the modern UFO era, a time of explanations, theories – and UFO investigators! – really began.

FILE STATUS

Unexplained; probably an atmospheric phenomenon
related to ball lightning or static electricity.

Close Encounters of the First Kind

Many strange objects had been seen in the sky previously. However, ufologists tend to fix the very first sighting of the modern UFO era as that of Kenneth Arnold on 24 June 1947. It wasn't the only sighting that day, and several had been reported earlier that week. What it did manage to do, however, was to get reported across the United States and the world; and it sparked off the imagination of the public. Before it, belief in UFOs, and especially the possibility that they were alien craft, was mainly confined to interested experts. After it, everyone knew what a flying saucer was.

Casebook: Kenneth Arnold

On that day in 1947, Kenneth Arnold was flying home in his single-engine plane over the Cascade Mountains in Washington State, USA. He was 32, a businessman and an experienced pilot, so it was no surprise that he decided to take a small diversion to see if he could spot a wrecked Marine Corps C-46 transport plane which had crashed recently.

As he banked over the small town of Mineral, about 40 kilometres from Mount Rainier, he was dazzled by a bright, blue-white flash. At first he thought it must have

Kenneth Arnold, whose 1947 sighting began the modern age of UFOs.

been a reflection off another plane, perhaps an Air Force Mustang buzzing him. As he looked around, he saw another flash and then, to the north and left of him, a most amazing sight: nine silvery, crescent-shaped discs were flying in a long line. The objects were following the contours of the mountains, and every so often one or another would dip slightly, causing the Sun to flash off it. Comparing their course with the landscape, he estimated that they were strung out over perhaps eight kilometres, and appeared to be travelling at around 1900 kilometres per hour! The strange craft crossed his path and he could clearly see that they had no tails. As they flew, they continued to bob and weave; later he said they were like 'speedboats in rough water'. It was obvious that they were something strange. They flew off, out of sight, and a troubled Arnold made for Yakima Air Base.

At first, he told the flight controllers when he landed, they might have been a secret type of aircraft, which he hoped was American rather than Russian. A fellow pilot suggested that they were guided missiles from the nearby Moses Lake testing range – but crescent-shaped? Eventually Arnold set off for his destination, Pendleton, Oregon. When he got there, he found that the controllers at Yakima had mentioned his strange sighting and word had got out: reporters were waiting, and Arnold gladly told them his story.

Next morning, the Seattle *Post-Intelligencer* bore the headline 'MYSTERY DISKS HURTLING ACROSS THE SKY'. The story was picked up and was soon being beamed to newspapers around the world. There was much debate across America. Most analysts were respectful: Arnold, although an experienced pilot, must have been mistaken in what he saw; he witnessed a mirage or an optical illusion. As the story spread, and a proper explanation still couldn't be found, the pilot was dismissed as a crackpot and a hoaxer. Arnold eventually admitted that he wished he'd kept the story to himself.

If he had, that wouldn't have been an end to the matter. There were eight other sightings in the same State that day, and twenty more over the next few days. UFO fever began to spread across America. By the end of 1947, over 850 sightings had been publicized, and the Air Force was forced to institute Project Sign to collect and examine all such reports.

So what did he see? It's probably too late to tell now. Some have suggested a secret test of the then-new Republic XP-84 Thunderjet. More recently, earthlights released from the mountains have offered another explanation (see page 37). It's all guesswork, however, and no one really knows.

FILE STATUS
Unexplained

'Flying saucers'

Ultimately, the real significance of Arnold's sighting was not what he saw, or said he saw, but what people thought he saw. Arnold's words were, 'They flew like a saucer would if you skipped it across the water.' Bill Bequette, a reporter for the *East Oregonian*, picked up that sentence and condensed it, and in the process he coined the phrase 'flying saucer'. Arnold's craft, of course, were tailless crescents, not saucers. The modern UFO age was only a few hours old and the truth had already been distorted. Not a good sign.

Sightings and more sightings

The files are full of UFO sightings; every year, more than 10,000 are reported from around the world. Most of them, it must be said, have a perfectly natural explanation, and in the next section we'll explain how that can be; but there are some which do not. That first year after Kenneth Arnold's sighting, there were dozens which remain unexplained to this day: grey spheres over Williams Field, Arizona; a yellow-white spherical craft flying over the Mojave Desert; a sky-blue saucer over Smoke River Canyon, Idaho; seven blue discs seen by a farmer in Rockfield, Wisconsin; eighteen white, oval UFOs witnessed by a bus driver in Clarion, Iowa. The list goes on and on.

Multiply it by 50 years, and add thousands of reports from every country in the world, and that's a heck of a lot of UFOs flying around. Surely they cannot all be correct? The Earth would have to be under invasion from several hundred different alien races, flying a veritable armada of various-shaped spacecraft. Some of the witnesses have to be mistaken – yet many cases remain unexplained.

© Fortean Picture Library

UFO photograph by schoolboy Stepen Pratt at Conisbrough, south Yorkshire, on 28 March 1966.

Casebook: The Washington waves

To illustrate this, a classic case occurred when aliens decided to demonstrate their existence to the most powerful man in the world by buzzing the White House in Washington, DC! It was back in 1952, in the middle of the most astonishing world-wide wave of UFO sightings. At times it seemed as if the planet must be under invasion from space, so numerous were the reports from the USA, Europe and Australia. Then, for two days at the end of July, the aliens' attention seemed to focus on America's capital city.

On the 19th, radar picked up eight unidentified craft flying at unbelievable speeds over the city. Airline pilots began radio-ing in sightings of lights; when military jets arrived to investigate, the objects disappeared, only to return once the planes had gone. While the jets were away chasing about over the city, a giant orange ball of light hovered over Andrews Air Force Base. These were very playful UFOs!

A week later, on the 26th, they came back for more fun. Between six and twelve UFOs dodged and wove over Washington, witnessed by dozens of people and clearly visible on radar. When the military jets arrived, the lights and radar traces blinked out just as before, then they popped back up the moment the planes had passed by. However, a second wave of jets turned up a couple of hours later, and this time one was surrounded by a circle of large, white balls. While the pilot was waiting for permission to shoot at them, they flew away and did not return. That didn't stop the jets from patrolling overhead for many more weeks; the whole city was gripped by UFO fever and many more unsubstantiated sightings were made.

The US Air Force's immediate explanation for all the UFOs and their odd behaviour was given as 'temperature inversions', strange weather conditions that can affect navigational instruments and give false readings. But can they create lights that weave around in the sky at high speed? It seems unlikely.

FILE STATUS
Unexplained

World-wide UFOs

In a strange follow-up to that case, Washington was also the scene of a flap for three weeks at the end of 1964, but this time the military were very tight-lipped about the sightings and their responses to them. They had obviously learnt to keep all discussion of UFOs and spacecraft secret.

In Europe, matters were much the same. After initial open speculation about strange sightings, the military in Britain and elsewhere began to keep news of them under wraps. There was the additional complication that serving armed forces personnel were bound by the Official Secrets Act and so could not publicize sightings without permission. The official explanation was always that there was no threat, that there were no UFOs and that there was a logical reason for every reported sighting. That did not stop them from happening.

Britain, especially, seemed particularly prone to sightings. At RAF Lakenheath and RAF Bentwaters near Ipswich, in Suffolk, in August 1956 they were apparently buzzed one whole evening by a radar-visible UFO, which was then also spotted from above by the crew of an American transport plane. Finally, a fast Venom fighter managed to get on the tail of the object, which was like a large glowing ball of light. The fighter pilot managed to get a 'lock' on to the object with his radar – there was definitely something solid there. Then the UFO flipped over and finished up *behind* the fighter plane. As a second Venom joined the chase, the UFO sped away northwards and disappeared. There was plenty of first-hand evidence, and even a short piece of film from the Venom's gun camera showing a fuzzy light. No wonder even the American report into UFOs, the usually sceptical Condon Report (see page 95), put it down to 'a mechanical device of unknown origin'!

And still the strange sightings continued. Hundreds of individual sightings continued to be reported, as they do to the present day. More dramatically, a major flap over Warminster, in Wiltshire, began in 1965, with strange lights continuing to be spotted by fans who flocked there to skywatch for several years.

Various British and American servicemen were startled by something very strange in Rendlesham Forest in Suffolk in December 1980; it could have been a peculiar military exercise – or it could have been a spacecraft touching down (see page 122 for more details). In 1990, southern England shared, with Belgium, a whole series of sightings of a mysterious, slow-moving, black triangle that seemed to pose such a threat it was even investigated by the

Belgian Government (see page 117 for the full story). And at the time of writing, UFOs in the form of mysterious bright lights continue to buzz the small Scottish town of Bonnybridge, with no proper explanation yet forthcoming.

Aeroplanes seem to provide the best opportunity for chance UFO sightings, by both crew and passengers. Throughout the summer of 1991 various airliners flying in and out London reported seeing small, unknown objects flying alongside them. In February 1996, an airliner coming in to land at Manchester Airport was buzzed by a large, black, triangular-shaped craft. The Joint Air Miss Working Group investigated but could find no acceptable explanation. The causes were never discovered and all were marked 'Unknown'. There are times when even the experts cannot explain a sighting.

Hoaxes & Fakes

On the other hand, some UFO cases are easily explained. Hoaxes have been tried since the time of the mystery airships. By now, investigators are used to them and know what to spot. In earlier days, though, the so-called experts were caught out time and again.

The case of British schoolboy, Alex Birch, is typical. In 1962 he claimed to have snapped five saucers flying over some trees near his house. His photograph certainly looked authentic. He was interviewed by the Ministry of Defence (MoD) and on television. His story was so convincing that he was even invited to speak at a meeting of BUFORA, the British UFO Research Association. It all seemed to be a genuine mystery. Ten years later, unable to keep the joke to himself any longer, Alex Birch revealed how he'd faked the picture: he'd just painted some vague UFO shapes on his bedroom window and photographed them against the background outside! All those experts must have felt very silly.

These days most fakes are found out instantly – yet still people try to get away with it. Why do people fake UFO photos? Some are mischievous, sure, but others just want the attention that a sighting brings. Others genuinely see something, but they believe they need real evidence to back up their claim to a sceptical world. Several famous photos from 1966, taken in Venezuela by one Inake Oses, fooled experts for years – until he confessed he'd faked them purely to get revenge on some ufologist friends who'd scorned him for not believing in flying saucers.

The advent of computer analysis has turned up yet more fakes. The high-tech Ground Saucer Watch computers examined over 700 photographs and found only 38 that were potentially unexplained. That's not to say that they really were UFOs: the experts just couldn't say for sure that they were a hoax. The trouble is that many of even the best UFO photos look as if someone has painted in the UFO and re-photographed the picture, or has simply lobbed a hub-cap or a lampshade into the air and snapped it. Even if people are genuinely sure they caught a UFO on film, it's hard to get such shots confirmed as real. Blurry pictures are too vague to be proved either way – but pin-sharp images have always been disregarded as 'too good to be true'. You can't win!

Casebook: Billy Meier

Someone who has always seemed too good to be true is Swiss farmhand Edward 'Billy' Meier. Since 1975 he has issued more than 600 crystal-clear photographs of flying saucers which he claims to have photographed. He also claims he has been in contact with their occupants, beautiful humanoids from the Pleiades who brought him a message of peace. At first such encounters were moderately logical, but later Meier claimed that he'd been given a ride in one of the spaceships, on a journey back through time to see dinosaurs, and forward to see San Francisco sinking into the bay after a devastating earthquake.

Contact with these beings, he said, ended in 1978, but he still claims to exchange telepathic messages with the Pleiadeans!

Being so numerous and so clear, Billy Meier's photographs have always been regarded with suspicion. One book on Meier was called *The Most Infamous Hoax in Ufology*. Ground Saucer Watch technology group did computer enhancements and were able to pinpoint strings holding up models. One sequence of pictures shows a saucer circling a tree. Unfortunately for Meier, when investigators went to the site, there was no tree: it had been superimposed on ordinary photos of the area, along with the model UFO it was holding up! Partially burnt test photos showing models used in some of the photos were found on Meier's farm, but Meier himself said that they were made later, inspired by his actual encounters. He always claimed that his incredible photos were real, and they continue to be published as genuine, or at least as 'possibles', around the world.

FILE STATUS
Hoax

Watch the Skies

The term 'UFO', standing for Unidentified Flying Object, is a somewhat confusing one. You mention it to people who aren't clued up on the subject, and they will immediately think of flying saucers piloted by little green men. This isn't at all accurate.

'UFO' means any aerial object or phenomenon that its witnesses cannot explain. This could be a strange fireball or type of meteor, an odd-shaped cloud-formation, a flock of flying pigs – or a genuine fleet of invading battlecruisers from Zeta Reticuli. Most UFOs are natural events, far removed from any science-fiction explanation. If you're feeling picky today, 'flying' can include something that is falling from the sky, or even a device that has landed, of course.

In fact, the real meaning of 'UFO' has become so distorted in the popular imagination that a newer term, UAP – unidentified atmospheric phenomenon – has been adopted by ufologists to cover all those sightings which plainly aren't the clichéd UFOs (i.e. alien spaceships). It's a little more of a mouthful, but it cuts down on the Little Green Men jokes. A bit.

Skywatching

Whatever you call them, though, it is certain that there are many puzzling things to be seen by anyone who has the patience to watch long enough. We'll run through all of them in the next few pages. But that's the main problem with skywatching – the amount of time it takes to actually see anything that might even remotely fit the heading of 'mildly interesting'. If you think fishing is boring, waiting hours and hours for a half-centimetre-long minnow to stumble on to your hook, perhaps skywatching is not for you. More than anything, it requires patience. Having a passion for astronomy will help, for a great deal of the time you'll be examining the stars (see the chart on page 35). Here are some other things you'll need:

A good spot: The best place to go looking for UFOs is one where other people have also observed something recently. Places which feature a lot of UFO activity are called *window areas*, and there's a section covering some of the most famous examples, both in Britain and elsewhere, later in this book. Typically, many of them are in very remote spots, which isn't very helpful. Skywatching at one of these places is likely to require a properly arranged trip and adult supervision.

You don't need to go out into the wilds just to watch

the skies, though. Sitting in your garden or looking out through your bedroom window (watch out for reflections!) will do almost as well. Ideally, you want to be somewhere where the sky is dark – that is, away from the lights of a town or roads, so that you can see as many stars as possible. The centre of London is not a good place for this. Obviously you don't want too many clouds to be obscuring the sky (let alone rain or snow!). Wherever you are, though, keep one eye on the sky and you never know what you might see!

A safe spot: Don't wander off anywhere without asking permission first, especially at night. It's just as much fun, say, to camp out in the back garden with a few fellow investigators and watch the skies while swapping spooky stories. You'll need to be warm, so it's probably best to save an outdoor skywatch for the summer holidays.

Equipment: Make sure you have all the necessary kit noted on page 7. Have binoculars or a telescope for everyone present, if you can. If anything does happen, you don't want to be fighting one another for a view! Bring along something comfy to sit on, and plenty of things to keep you amused. Plan it right, and a skywatch can be great fun.

Unidentified?

With only a pinch of common sense, most UFOs quickly turn into *IFOs* – Identified Flying Objects. In fact, it has been worked out that anything up to about 95 per cent of all sightings can be explained. The trouble with that figure is not the 95 per cent – it's the 5 per cent that cannot yet be explained.

Of course, the fact that a sighting cannot be explained does not immediately prove the existence of alien spacecraft and the like. Many of the explanations for the stranger types of atmospheric phenomena have been discovered only in the last couple of decades – indeed, odd events like ball lightning are not yet proven, though that one has, at last, been accepted by many scientists as a possibility. In other words, it may not be possible to explain some UFOs at present – but only because we don't yet know everything. Some people are very keen to believe in the existence of alien craft, so they'd rather assume that an inexplicable sighting was proof of such things than admit that they just don't know.

The spotter's guide to common UFOs

Amidst all the weird clouds, mistaken planets, mist-shrouded meteor showers and the others we'll discuss over the page, it must be admitted that there are people who have seen distinctly spacecraft-shaped UFOs. These pesky things come in all shapes and sizes, from giant ping-pong balls to tiny rotating discs. Does this mean that there are many different species of alien buzzing Earth at any one time, or could it be that some of the witnesses are mistaken? Perhaps you should try to find out.

UFO Types Chart

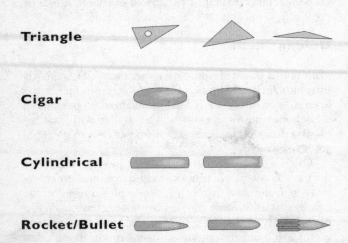

Triangle

Cigar

Cylindrical

Rocket/Bullet

Boomerang

**Manta/
Bird Shape**

Elliptical

Spherical

Flat Bottom

Cone-topped

Lens-shaped

**Lens
& Dome**

Flat Disc

Is it a bird, a plane . . .?

You can divide the sorts of things people mistake for UFOs into two general categories: either human-made items, both piloted and unmanned, or natural phenomena, from shooting stars to peculiar weather-patterns.

There is an awful lot of man-made stuff flying or floating about up there: satellites, planes, helicopters, gliders, kites – if it flies, someone's mistaken it for a UFO. The craze for promotional airships and odd-shaped balloons has been responsible for more sightings, particularly those which are lit up at night with neon advertising slogans. Rock festivals with giant laser light-shows and common firework displays have also been cited. To be honest, though, all it sometimes takes are aeroplane lights, a foggy night and *Close Encounters* on the TV again – and, lo and behold: another rash of UFO sightings gets logged.

It has long been known that certain aircraft, particularly the huge US bombers, look very much like flat, UFO-ish oblongs when seen from the side. More recently it has been suggested that tests of the secret Stealth aircraft, those sinister, black flying-wing-shaped aircraft that are invisible to radar, may have triggered UFO flaps in various parts of the world. These surveillance craft occasionally need to do practice runs at very low altitudes, and of course the Americans would never admit to having a secret plane that no one was supposed to know about. The Stealth bomber and fighter have both been flown in public now, but there are repeated rumours about the new Aurora craft, allegedly a large black triangle in shape, that seems to be causing yet more sightings. Less excitingly, when aircraft refuel in mid-air, they can appear to form strange shapes: these have also caused many sightings.

Not all man-made objects that are mistaken for UFOs are as large or as technologically advanced as a Stealth bomber. Recently, an ordinary household bin-liner caused a panic in the West Midlands when various witnesses reported a slow-moving dark object gliding across the sky! And if you think that's daft, we'd better not mention the glowing owl that fooled a couple of skywatchers in Northamptonshire. It turned out that it had eaten phosphorescent fungi which literally made it glow in the dark!

Space oddities

Just because NASA or another space agency sends a satellite high into orbit, that doesn't mean it's never going to come back down again. Pieces of space junk are burning up in the atmosphere quite regularly. There is a famous case, from December 1978, when the emergency services across much of Europe were alerted about a crashed aircraft. Two hundred witnesses swore that they had seen a long fuselage plummeting down, fire streaming behind it. There was no crash: it was a Soviet space probe breaking up in Earth's atmosphere. Several burning pieces had spread out in a line, causing observers to assume that they were seeing a row of lighted windows! These days, when a major piece of junk is coming back the scientists tend to warn everybody (remember the Chinese satellite that fell back to Earth early in 1996?), but there are thousands of smaller fragments burning up all the time.

Up in orbit, too, observers have mistaken natural and man-made phenomena for something more peculiar. There was a famous example when the astronauts aboard Apollo 11 reported seeing inexplicable glowing objects, and they even managed to take a blurry photo. The objects turned out to be clusters of water globules ejected from their own craft during a previous orbit, and the photo was of a Russian satellite that had been launched a few years earlier.

An odd little corner of ufology is devoted to the study of astronaut-to-base messages, and this has produced outlandish claims that various astronauts on the Apollo missions have sent coded messages reporting seeing spacecraft and even alien cities on the Moon. 'Coded', you'll notice: as far as the records show, at least, no astronaut ever reported anything so incredible in plain speech. If there really were strange artefacts found on the Moon, the

Americans would still be sending missions there, wouldn't they? Sure, unless they were too scared to go back, a believer might reply.

Lost in the stars

The first thing any 'expert' is likely to say when asked to explain a strange light seen in the sky is this: the planet Venus. Or, failing that, the Moon, Mars, Jupiter or Saturn. At certain times of the year, these planets, and particularly Venus, hang low over the horizon, shining brightly in the reflected light of the rising or setting Sun. Add a little haze or low cloud which makes the glowing disc seem far larger than usual, with the clouds shifting suddenly to give the illusion that the light is moving about, and you've got a classic UFO that has been reported a thousand times. There is even a story that during the Second World War a US Navy battleship fired round after round of ammunition at Venus, in the belief that it was the enemy!

Meteors are generally small fragments of rocky matter that circle the Sun. Usually when they hit the Earth's atmosphere they burn up with a bright light that can sometimes be seen from the ground. These are called shooting stars; occasionally you get a few dozen pieces all together, causing a shower of glittering lights. Keep your eyes open on the clearest nights, and you may see some too. Very occasionally, pieces get as far as Earth's inner atmosphere before exploding; a few even hit the ground; these are meteorites. Larger meteorites are far rarer, though they do hit our planet infrequently. The largest definite proof of a meteorite strike is Meteor Crater in Arizona, more than 2.5 kilometres across, formed 30,000 years ago!

Comets, larger blazing masses which circle the Solar System in great looping arcs, are far rarer. The most famous, Halley's Comet, comes around every 76 years or so; the next occurrence will not be until 2062. About a dozen comets are tracked annually, with one visible from Earth only every few years.

The sky at night

Being a skywatcher invariably involves also developing an interest in astronomy, as all that time staring at the heavens pays off. This star map shows all the major constellations which can be seen above Britain (those nearest the edges may be visible only in the summer or winter). Using it, you should quickly be able to spot if something very bright is in the wrong place!

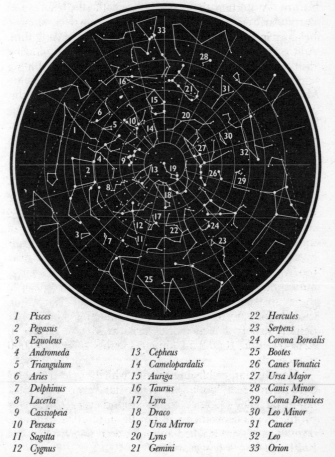

1	Pisces		
2	Pegasus		
3	Equoleus		
4	Andromeda	13	Cepheus
5	Triangulum	14	Camelopardalis
6	Aries	15	Auriga
7	Delphinus	16	Taurus
8	Lacerta	17	Lyra
9	Cassiopeia	18	Draco
10	Perseus	19	Ursa Mirror
11	Sagitta	20	Lyns
12	Cygnus	21	Gemini
		22	Hercules
		23	Serpens
		24	Corona Borealis
		25	Bootes
		26	Canes Venatici
		27	Ursa Major
		28	Canis Minor
		29	Coma Berenices
		30	Leo Minor
		31	Cancer
		32	Leo
		33	Orion

Weird weather

Closer to home, there are all manner of freaky weather conditions which can trigger UFO sightings. Among the most famous are *lenticular clouds*. These are solid, round-edged formations, created where layers of warm and cold air meet, and they do, it must be said, look very like the classic flying saucer shape. *Noctilucent clouds* are tiny clusters of vapour gathered around dust and they stay very high in the atmosphere – where they catch the last rays of the setting Sun and glow brightly against the dark evening sky. These cloud types are rare, though; perhaps if they were more common everybody would be more used to them and be less inclined to think they were spaceships!

Both clouds and fog can distort the light of the Sun or Moon, making it appear strange, even moving. In the upper atmosphere, ice crystals distort sunlight further. Sun dogs or mock Suns, more properly called *parhelia*, are reflections of sunlight on tiny ice fragments which make it look as if there were several more glowing balls in view. They are often observed by people in high aeroplanes, especially at sunset, and have been widely photographed – which isn't to say they don't still confuse people! You

© Fortean Picture Library

Lenticular clouds over Mt Shasta, Northern California, USA, 1980 – definitely not flying saucers.

don't even need ice crystals to cause reflections; some low cloud will reflect lights as ordinary as car headlamps or streetlights. One famous low-flying UFO turned out to be the lights of a hotel on a distant hillside seen through low cloud.

In extreme northerly and southerly locations, brightly scintillating *aurora* such as the Aurora Borealis are regular features of the skies. These glowing sheets of light are caused by charged particles from the Sun, attracted by the Earth's magnetic field, glowing as they burn up in the outer atmosphere. Less fantastically, a researcher in an aeroplane reported seeing something very similar to Kenneth Arnold's silver spaceships flying in formation: they turned out to be frozen raindrops seen through the thick layers of glass of the plane's window!

Great balls of fire

Ball lightning has been blamed for UFO sightings for some time, but only recently has it been recognized by science. It shows itself as a bizarre ball of glowing energy, in size between a tennis ball and a football, and it can apparently pass through windows and doors. Most commonly found after a lightning strike, ball lightning will fizz and hum as it glides through the air in an almost intelligent manner. Unlike lightning, though, it won't give anyone it hits a massive shock.

Originally ball lightning was thought to be nothing more than a mass hallucination – until one example floated down the aisle of an aeroplane in March 1963, right before the eyes of an electronics professor! Now there have been more than 600 recorded sightings, and it is a recognized, if rare, scientific phenomenon.

Earthlights and skylights

Strange lights have long been reported around the sites of earthquakes, both before and after tremors. In the last decade, experts such as Paul Devereux have finally discovered why. It seems that some rocks under great pressure can emit energy or hot ionized gas which glows when it reaches the air, creating *earthlights*. The Tectonic Stress Theory is still being developed, but it may explain why some hilly areas have more than their fair share of strange lights and UFO sightings.

Finally, even more recently scientists have discovered why pilots flying at high altitudes have always claimed to see bizarre flashing lights near thunderstorms. In 1989, researchers finally managed to videotape a few of these lights, and what a revelation they were! Now there is little doubt about the *blue jets* and *red sprites* that leap out from the crowns of thunderstorms. They can look like spikes or columns, wavering blobs or multi-armed octopuses, and they can shoot as far as 90 kilometres into space at immense speeds! Jets and sprites have been reported by observers on the ground for more than a century but, until now, they have always been put down to reflections or after-images left by lightning. Yet again, science has finally managed to explain a mysterious UFO event.

Raining sprats and frogs

There are some things, though, which have, as yet, evaded a rational explanation – even if everyone has his or her own theories. But how can it be that live fish, frogs, crabs and a whole variety of inanimate objects fall from the sky?

Strange falls have been recorded since the time of the Ancient Greeks, and they continue to be reported from all corners of the globe. Most commonly, the items tend to be small and light, giving rise to the belief that they have been picked up by the wind or a waterspout. In 1979, tiny frogs no bigger than a 50p piece rained down on a Bedfordshire village. Something similar happened in Stroud, Gloucestershire, in October 1987; this time, the frogs were an unusual pink colour, which allowed them to be traced back to their natural habitat: the deserts of North Africa! Could they have been swept up by a tornado or just a hearty gust of wind, and carried for 2000 kilometres before falling – and fall gently enough not to be killed? Certainly it has been proved that sand and dust from the Sahara fall over wide areas of Europe two or three times a year.

However, frogs can often emerge after a rainfall anyway, which lends some doubt to the 'carried off' theory. But what about the tiny fish that were found, flipping about on a roof after a shower in east London, in May 1984? Something similar happened in Thirsk, Yorkshire, a month later, with a fall of starfish and winkles! If it was a waterspout, one of those strange whirling columns of water formed like a whirlwind, which transported them so far, why didn't it pick up and deposit pebbles, seaweed or other plants?

And even if you can accept that a waterspout or a violent storm might pick up a few tiny fish, what could possibly explain the three umbrellas which fell out of a clear sky over Durban, South Africa, in late 1980? There are some things that will, perhaps, remain unexplained for ever!

Ice bombs away

On the other hand, it seems as if a related phenomena are well on the way to being explained. *Ice bombs* are large, all-too-solid hunks of frozen ice which have smashed their way through house roofs and have dented cars after falling from the sky! Again, such falls have been recorded for many centuries – which rather puts paid to the explanation that they are falling from aircraft. Certainly there have been cases when ice – or, worse, something noxious from a faulty toilet! – has fallen to Earth from a plane, but that could hardly have happened 100 years ago.

The largest ice bomb ever recorded was over 1.6 metres wide and weighed more than 75 kilograms. It smashed in the roof of a house in Devon in June 1984. Many more falls have been reported, from all parts of the world. However, the breakthrough came when, following a bolt of lightning, a large ice bomb narrowly missed a scientist, Dr R. S. Griffiths, in a Manchester street in April 1973. An expert on storms, he gathered up a huge chunk. Studying it in his lab, he managed to find that it was built up with layer upon layer of ice, rather like a hailstone but much bigger. Like a hailstone, he suggested, it could have formed high above the ground among the same fields of ice crystals that cause Sun dogs. But this ice bomb was twice the size of a football – could it really have avoided the effects of gravity for so long?

It has been suggested that at least some ice bombs may in fact be *ice comets*. Scientists have detected the presence of frozen water (which is, after all, just hydrogen and oxygen combined) in comets. Perhaps, just as there are rocky meteorites, there could be similar clusters made of ice. More study is required, but it plainly demonstrates just how many odd phenomena can be found up in the air, even without all those alien spacecraft!

If You See a UFO

As the last few pages have detailed, most of what are initially thought to be UFOs can easily be explained as strange weather, stars or odd aircraft. If you should see something that you really cannot explain, however, here's what you should do.

Get a record: Firstly, try to get it on film, as many shots as you can. Try, amidst all the panic, to stay calm and get clear shots, in focus and with that darn lens cap off. If you can, frame the object against other recognizable landmarks, such as a tree or people, so it will be possible to work out how big it might have been.

If you don't have a camera to hand, draw a sketch as quickly as possible after the sighting; if it moved, draw several. You don't need to be Leonardo da Vinci, but include as many details as you can recall.

Write down everything that happened. Try to include the speed, direction, colour, shape and angle of the object, every last detail; include senses other than your sight, such as any strange smells, or a change of temperature. Also describe the weather conditions, the time and whether any other people were present. Make sure you have a record of the exact location.

If you believe something landed, find out whether there's any evidence from the landing site, such as indentations or burn marks. Capture them on film or as further sketches. Try not to disturb anything.

Get other witnesses: The more people who see any object, the more chance you have of being taken seriously. Get them to take photos, make drawings and write down their own account too. A record of their names and addresses will also help.

This is important: keep their accounts separate. Try not to discuss with them the details of what happened until they have written their own story down. It's too easy for someone to say, for example, 'No, it was taller than that, and grey rather than black'; before you know it, you'll be changing your story because you've started to doubt it, and the truth will have been lost.

Tell people: This part may prove the trickiest, or at least somewhat embarrassing. If you are pretty certain that what you saw was not an IFO, and you're prepared to stand by your story (and perhaps even risk being branded a bit of a weirdo), contact the authorities. In most cases this will be the local police (don't dial 999; use their regular number – unless it really is an emergency, of course!) or, more likely, a nearby airport or RAF base. Don't worry about sounding like a right twit; in most cases they'll even be able to tell you what it really was you just saw.

If you want to, submit a sighting report to a reputable UFO investigation group, such as BUFORA. (There are contact addresses at the back of this book.) They will want as much detail as you can give them. They may have heard from other witnesses, and again they may already have a logical explanation for you.

When telling other people, you don't have to inform them that you actually believe in UFOs. All you need say, if you prefer, is that you saw (or even took photos of) something you don't understand, and you would like to share it with other people in the hope that they may provide a satisfactory explanation. Try *not* to get a photograph of yourself on the front of the local newspaper dressed up like Captain Kirk or a Dalek. That won't help anyone take you seriously.

One final word: just to repeat what we said earlier, don't make hoax reports or fake photos. Hoaxers always get found out, sooner or later, and, boy, do they look *stupid* when that happens.

Close Encounters of the Second Kind

If you just see a strange shape in the sky, there is little to prove that this is, in fact, an alien craft. If it moves like a vehicle, changes direction and speeds up or slows down, that's more proof. But if it causes weird things to happen, like making your watch stop, and if it then takes off, leaving huge scorch marks on your front lawn, that's evidence which can go a long way to proving or disproving what it was.

The effects that UFOs can have on people are many and varied. At their simplest, they may release static electricity, which causes your hair to stand up and metal surfaces to give off sparks. Witnesses have talked of a 'cone of silence', a totally quiet area underneath a hovering UFO in which no noise can be heard. Vehicles and other devices have been stopped, sometimes permanently, apparently affected by alien craft. Never mind your watch stopping: some UFOs appear to cause people to lose hours, though this is more usually associated with abduction experiences.

Casebook: Captain Mantell

Possibly the earliest apparent CE2K happened only six months after Kenneth Arnold's momentous sighting. On 7 January 1948, State police in Maysville, Kentucky, USA, spotted an enormous UFO shaped like a 'silver teardrop' heading straight for Goodman Air Force Base, near Fort Knox. A warning was relayed to base commander Colonel Guy Hix. Four minutes later, he and six others watched as the metallic-looking object, described variously as looking like 'an upside-down ice-cream cone' and 'umbrella-shaped', hovered over the airfield.

Three Army F-51 fighters scrambled in pursuit of the craft. Their leader, Captain Thomas Mantell, soon had 'that thing' in his sights. It rose higher and higher into the sky, and Mantell followed it. At around 7000 metres the other planes broke off and returned to base, but Mantell radioed to the control tower to state that he was continuing. The ground lost sight of his plane and there were no further messages.

Captain Thomas Mantell Jr

A search started almost immediately, and the wreckage of his plane was found strewn over a five-kilometre area later that afternoon. The media hounded the Air Force for an explanation and, desperate to appear efficient, it gave them one. Captain Mantell had been chasing the planet Venus, they said, and had run out of oxygen. This was plainly ludicrous; there were a great many reliable witnesses to the strange craft, and Venus is rarely visible at all in a clear afternoon sky.

It wasn't until five years later that a far better explanation emerged. Declassified documents revealed that secret Navy Skyhook spy balloons were being launched from Camp Ripley, Minnesota, without the knowledge of the Army. These craft, 130 metres tall and 30 metres across, certainly tally with the witness reports from Goodman. Why an experienced pilot like Mantell carried on chasing the balloon until he ran out of oxygen has not been explained.

Despite such a likely cause, and with no real evidence to support it, a legend grew among ufologists that a brave pilot had been shot down by a UFO. The military, it said, was hiding the real truth and all pilots were being instructed to treat flying saucers as hostile. Calls came for the US military to stop shooting at the saucers, which were plainly only firing back in self-defence! Early contactee George Adamski (see page 58) said later that he had been told by his Venusian friends that they deeply regretted the whole episode. Mantell had apparently been affected by the power field of a large, manned spacecraft – but you'll have to read the section on Adamski to decide whether that is anything like a believable explanation.

FILE STATUS

Misidentified Skyhook balloon.

Casebook: Betty Cash

Captain Mantell's tragic crash appears, in the end, not to have been due to the effects of a UFO. The case of Betty Cash is very different indeed, for it resulted in very specific, witnessed injuries – and has a troubling outcome.

It was around nine, on the evening of 29 December 1980. Betty Cash, her friend, Vicky Landrum, and the latter's young grandson, Colby, were driving through the woods near Huffman, Texas, USA. Suddenly, a fiery object appeared in the sky. It was roughly diamond-shaped, with a row of blue dots around its middle, and flames shot out from its underside. It descended in front of their car until it was hovering, maybe 50 metres away. The three got out of the car and stared at the craft, which just hung there, the roaring of its flames accompanied by a beeping noise.

Colby was scared and began crying, so he and his grandmother jumped back into the car. When Betty made to join them, she found that the door-handle was scorching hot. The craft moved away ahead of them and they followed it from what they hoped was a safe distance. As they did so, they noticed a great many helicopters in the sky all around the craft. One, a CH-47 twin-engined Chinook, flew right over the road, and in all Betty counted 23 aircraft around the UFO.

When they eventually arrived home, all three witnesses were in a terrible state. Betty developed blinding headaches, neck pains, skin irritation and sickness. Colby appeared to have a badly sunburnt face, and over the next few days both Vicky and Betty lost hair. Betty's eyes became swollen and she could not see. All three spent a long time in hospital in Houston. A definite diagnosis could not be made, but it was plain that they had been exposed to some strong source of radiation.

The presence of those helicopters around the UFO seemed to indicate that the whole affair was a military operation, so Cash and Landrum sued the US Government for $20 million. When the case came to court, however, representatives from the Army, Air Force, Navy and NASA all testified that they didn't own or operate such a strange vehicle. No one admitted that any of their helicopters were in the area that night. The judge decided that as a result there was no case to be made, and in August 1986 it was dismissed. Neither Cash nor Landrum was allowed to testify, nor were several independent witnesses who had also seen the helicopters that night. Some ufologists have been very troubled by such an outcome, which doesn't seem to bode well for any further government 'openness' about UFOs.

As to what the craft actually was . . . well, as you can imagine, there are as many theories as there were helicopters. Among them: it was the test of a nuclear-powered space vehicle such as a space shuttle that went very wrong and was being escorted back to base. Less credibly, much has been made of the suggestion that it was a captured alien craft being test-flown in order to discover more about it. That may seem extremely unlikely, perhaps; however, without an official explanation by whoever owned those helicopters, that may be as good as it gets.

FILE STATUS

Unexplained — and rather scary.

Major malfunctions

There have been a small number of cases as serious as that of Betty Cash, all of them unexplained. While the mind can do many things, including causing the body to seem to be suffering from any number of diseases, radiation sickness and burns are probably beyond it. Thankfully, such events are rare.

Far more commonly, the presence of a UFO in the sky has been known to affect vehicles, either their electrics or their engines. In the case of truck driver Carl Farlow from Hampshire, in southern England, it wasn't so much a UFO as a UTO – an Unidentified Trundling Object. In November 1967, he was driving late at night along the A338 with a lorryload of kitchen equipment, when his lights spluttered and died. As his diesel-powered engine was unaffected, he pulled over to examine the truck's electrics. Before he could get out of the cab, he was astonished to see a huge, egg-shaped machine, maybe 25 metres across, trundle noisily across the road, making a loud grinding noise, before disappearing into the darkness. Where it had been, the surface of the road had melted. On the far side, another car had stopped, and its two passengers had also seen everything. Despite extensive investigation by the police and the Ministry of Defence, no explanation has ever been found for this singular encounter.

There is a whole catalogue of other effects caused by UFOs. Radios, easily affected by interference, fill with static. Metal surfaces get warm; paint blisters and wood chars. Most spookily, perhaps, bizarre fogs descend; within their shifting swirls witnesses lose hours or move to another location. For example, off the coast of Finland in July 1991 two men on holiday were cruising in a hired motor launch. A black sphere appeared in the sky, surrounded by flickering lights. One of the lights, larger than the rest, moved towards their vessel. The boat was surrounded by some kind of fog. One of the men found he couldn't move his neck. Then the lights all disappeared. As the fog lifted, the pair discovered that they were sitting in different seats from before and that, although seven and a half hours had gone by, their boat was still exactly where it had been before their mysterious, and still unexplained, encounter.

Casebook: Nullarbor

CE2K cases can often be the weirdest of all the types, as this further example proves. The place was Western Australia, on 21 January 1988. Fay Knowles, her three grown-up sons and two dogs, were driving from Perth towards Mundrabilla late at night. Around 1.30 a.m., their car radio was filled with interference. Fifteen minutes later they saw lights glowing in the distance. A car was stationary, and hanging above it was a glowing ball of light. Sean Knowles, driving, swerved to avoid the other vehicle, then he turned around to go back and investigate. The UFO chased their car – then something landed on the roof with a thump and the vehicle seemed to rise up in the air! Everyone felt very strange, and the dogs howled in fright. Dust swirled in through the window and there was a foul smell.

Then suddenly they were falling again. Their car fell to the ground with a crash, bursting a tyre. Sean managed to halt it safely, so they all jumped out and hid until the white light flew away. That was scary, but there was an oddly comical side-effect: for about 15 minutes after the encounter, everyone's voice was really squeaky and high-pitched, as if they'd all been inhaling helium. It was in that ludicrous state that they changed the tyre, looked worriedly at four new dents in the roof, then they drove on.

As usual, there have been suggestions that this was a hoax or, to be kinder, a hallucination brought on by driving late at night in the desert. Possibly the travellers just fell asleep. Maybe so – but that doesn't explain how a tuna fishing boat off the coast was also buzzed by a white light which left everyone speaking in a Mickey Mouse voice that very same night . . . (You may wish to sing the theme tune from *The Twilight Zone* at this point.)

FILE STATUS
Unexplained

Crop Circles

In recent years, a whole new area of the strange has opened up, and for a time it looked as if UFOs were the culprits. Crop circles, those peculiar patterns flattened out in cornfields, have really captured the public's imagination, bringing with them an explosion of wild theories. They have been reported across most of England, particularly the southern counties, but also as far afield as Australia, Canada and, especially, Japan.

The first modern crop circle was reported in the Wiltshire local press in the summer of 1980. A farmer near Westbury had come across a 20-metre circle impressed into one of his oat fields that May. He ploughed it in, but over the following months several

© Fortean Picture Library

Crop circles at Westbury, Wiltshire, 1988.

more appeared. What he found most peculiar about them was that the crop, although flattened, was not damaged and was continuing to grow. When the story was reported, a local UFO investigation group proposed that the circles were the pattern left after a saucer had landed. This idea, quite rightly perhaps, quickly drifted into obscurity.

Over the next few years, more circular patterns flattened into fields were reported, particularly in Wiltshire and Hampshire. Their peculiar unexplained nature led to them being examined by more ufologists, and several magazines ran articles on the mystery. In time, such stories started to be picked up by the national media. And then, once everyone knew about crop circles, they seemed to be popping up all over the place.

Initially, all these circles were just that: a plain, round area of flattened wheat or oats, with clearly defined edges and all the plants folded gently down, usually in a neat swirl. As the subject became more widely known, new shapes began to appear. At first they took the form of several circles linked by lines, and then curves; but pretty soon all manner of outlandish, hieroglyph-like patterns were appearing in fields. There was even one of those strange, bulbous Chaos Theory shapes, with each section's plants swirling into smaller and smaller circles.

These all served to attract yet more attention, for they were certainly strange and beautiful. Books and television shows were devoted to the subject; a flood of theories, from the sensible to the crackpot, were offered to explain them all. Crop-circle experts became known as *cereologists*. The new patterns turned up on T-shirts, adverts and record sleeves.

Prompted as much, perhaps, by their general strangeness as by reports of increased UFO activity in circle areas, experts from BUFORA, helped by weather experts from TORRA (Tornado and Storm Research Organization), began a long investigation. Looking back through the records, they discovered that circles had been reported by farmers for over a century. They had always been put down to a freak weather condition, such as a small whirlwind. Diligent research uncovered a very old report of a circle in Assen, Holland, from 1590!

More importantly, they found evidence of such formations in other parts of the world. Forty countries had reported examples of the new wave of crop circles, but almost all of them also had a history of simple circles forming in corn and the like. The countries included Russia, Canada and New Zealand. From Australia came the most important information. They had recorded circles regularly in the Mallee wheat belt in Victoria and South Australia since the early 1970s. There it had been suggested – half-jokingly – that they were kangaroo nests! Yet years before even these, a sugar-cane farmer from northern Queensland spoke of the day in January 1966 when he witnessed a dark oval of spiralling air form out of a bed of reeds before his very eyes. As it touched the sugar cane, it left a regular-shaped circle of bent-over crops. So was this the answer?

Crop circle theories

The first circles were regular round shapes. Something, or somebody, had pushed the corn down around a central point, leaving a circular depression in the middle of a field of high-standing plants. There was little question that such circles looked artificial: their edges were even and clearly defined, and the crop was usually flattened into an intricate swirl. But there appeared to be little real evidence of human presence: no footprints, no plants knocked over by people trampling through into the middle of a field, and nobody seen actually making a circle.

What some farmers *were* seeing were UFOs. Many crop circles appeared in areas where increased UFO activity was already being witnessed, particularly strange lights and noises. There were suggestions that the circles were caused by flying saucers landing. However, some circles were only a metre or so across, while the largest was more than three hundred times that size. Spacecraft, it was alleged, would leave burn or scorch marks from their engines, and they wouldn't have flattened the corn so precisely.

Just as bizarrely, other cereologists suggested that the patterns might be caused by deer or other animals making areas for their young to be born and reared in. There was even talk of frolicking hedgehogs – which, as you can imagine, some newspapers lapped up. Only a little more credibly, someone suggested that perhaps they were the site of long-removed standing-stone formations that were sinking back into their ancient shapes. Well, it was all very mystical, but not very likely. Nor was the idea that they were unexploded Second World War bombs going off under the ground. As they were better seen from the air, someone suggested, perhaps they were signalling to somebody, rather like the markings on the Nazca plains. Others talked of messages from an alien intelligence; but people just laughed at them and tapped their foreheads knowingly.

When the more complicated patterns began to appear, they were adapted into the theories, but as they grew more and more unlikely, it became obvious that most of them, if not all, were not being made by anything more mystical than a bunch of people having fun. Indeed, the realization that this was the explanation

almost meant that all circles were put down to hoaxers –
but was this really the case?

An expert in tornadoes and whirlwinds, Dr Terence
Meaden, proposed a new kind of wind vortex, similar to
a whirlwind, but unfortunately he tried to adapt it to
explain the complex hieroglyphic shapes as well.
However, his initial idea was expanded and studied, and
the reports of many eyewitnesses, including the
Australian sugar-cane farmer, were added to the equa-
tion.

It turned out that over 40 people had seen a rotating
air-mass form over fields on particularly warm days. The
swirl of air had often just broken up again, but on a few
occasions it had dipped to Earth. Where it touched the
corn, it left a simple circle of flattened crops before disin-
tegrating back into the surrounding air.

However, a number of these events were accompanied
by lights and humming or buzzing noises. These might
account for the apparent UFO sightings, but they could
not readily be explained by the simple whirlwind theory.
There had to be a different form of energy involved as
well, which is where the theory of a *plasma vortex* comes in.
Plasma is highly electrically-charged air which can cause
strange atmospheric effects. In a laboratory in Japan in
1994, scientists managed to produce a whirlwind of
charged air that swirled in a blue column before leaving a
circular mark on a photographic plate. Such experiments
are still continuing, but a theory has taken shape. Perhaps,
in the hot, dry summer air there is such a build-up of
static electricity that a small portion of the air above a
field becomes charged with plasma. Eventually this forms
into a whirlwind, just like the dust you see in a playground
or on the ground in a shopping centre. In a few cases,
maybe, this whirlwind grows so strong that it spins down
into the crop and flattens it. But this is still only a theory.

A hoax, you say?

What is not a theory, however, is that there have been
people in their hundreds out there making crop circles. It

was always an obvious explanation, even back in the days of the simple circles. By the time Mandelbrot sets, birds and all sorts of complicated, Spirograph-like patterns started appearing, it seemed likely to be the only answer.

But how could people possibly manage to make such neat circles, the cereologists argued. All that corn is flattened very carefully, and the swirls are so regular that surely they couldn't be made by a couple of people stumbling about in the dark after the pubs have shut. But in fact it was found to be fairly easy to create even the most complicated and neatest designs – as was confirmed in September 1991.

A major splash in *Today* newspaper declared that they had found the answer to all those pesky corn circles. Doug Bower and Dave Chorley, two retired artists, had come forward and declared that since 1980 they had made several hundred circles and more complicated patterns, inspired originally by those 1970s stories of the Australian kangaroo nests. What's more, they could prove it: a dozen of their most recent designs, they said, had included subtle double-D patterns in them – and, sure enough, there they were.

To prove that their designs could fool even the most ardent cereologist, Doug and Dave created a typical circle, which was then shown to circle expert Pat Delgado. He duly declared it genuine and was very shamefaced when it was proved to him that it was made by a couple of old men and a few planks.

Mind you, Delgado had been involved in other dubious declarations before. Six months earlier, in an attempt to film a circle being made, he and fellow cereologist Colin Andrew had initiated Operation Blackbird and had set up television cameras to watch likely fields in a series of night vigils. Eventually their patience was rewarded one night when strange lights on the horizon were captured by heat-sensing cameras and a complicated pattern appeared right in front of them. The word went out that final proof had been found – but in the morning light all they found was a crudely flattened hoax with an Ouija board left in its centre. The lights had been nothing more than the body-heat of the hoaxers who – the cereologists would have realized if they had read their *Smash Hits* the next week – were none other than pop mavericks The KLF promoting a new single!

Other hoaxing groups came out of the woodwork after *Today's* revelations. Doug and Dave said that all they used were simple planks of wood to flatten the corn and hide their footprints, and lengths of twine to help create a circle. Others now showed how they used blocks of polystyrene to avoid damaging the plants. Now there were Design-a-Crop-Circle competitions, and even more outlandish patterns, but the craze was dying away. In the last couple of years there have been far fewer hieroglyph-style patterns. They still appear, certainly, but now it is usually known who made them and how. And now that people are less interested in paying to visit such attractions, farmers are more concerned about their ruined crops.

The problem is this, though: the plain circles keep on being found, and no one is owning up to them. As cereologist Paul Fuller once put it, 'When the media stop promoting the phenomenon as a supernatural mystery, the hoaxers will go away and leave us with the real circles.' It seems like that has now started to happen.

© Fortean Picture Library

Crop circles at Cheesefoot Head near Winchester, Hampshire, 1993.

Tunguska

Crop circles may prove to be a purely Earthly phenomenon, but there is little doubt that whatever it was that exploded eight kilometres above the Earth's surface at the Tunguska region in Siberia, Russia – and created the largest 'crop circle' ever known – came from space.

In the summer of 1908, people all around the world witnessed strange lights in the sky and experienced various odd atmospheric conditions. Clouds and sunsets glowed with unearthly reds and purples, and in parts of Europe one could read a newspaper at midnight. Everywhere, strong seismic shockwaves were recorded from deepest Russia, as if caused by an earthquake.

However, it wasn't until 1921 that the facts began to emerge. A Soviet scientist, Leonid Kulik, was researching meteorite falls in Russia. He was told about a monster example that had allegedly landed in Siberia in 1908. Kulik gathered up eyewitness reports from the time. People in a village 300 kilometres from the explosion had seen an immense column of light streak down from a cloudless sky. When the shining ball reached the ground, somewhere over the valley of the Stony Tunguska River, a huge mushroom-shaped cloud formed and vast shockwaves swept across the region. Roofs burned and buildings were flattened, but luckily the isolated nature of the region had meant that no one died.

Kulik made several expeditions to the Tunguska region and was astonished by what he found. All the trees in every direction around the crash site for more than 30 kilometres had been flattened, and all in the same direction: outwards. It was a terrifying and eerie sight. But at the centre trees were still standing, albeit stripped of their branches – and there was no crater or any fragments of meteorite.

Theories galore

So what was it that had caused such devastation at Tunguska? There have been many theories down the years, and Russian scientists continue to study the area in search of a definitive answer.

In 1973, two Texan scientists suggested that it could have been a mini black hole, a tiny collapsed star that was little more than a ball of ferocious gravity. It could have passed right through the Earth and come out on the other side. But that would have meant it emerging somewhere between Iceland and Newfoundland, with a similar effect to what happened at Tunguska. Nothing like that happened.

That sinister mushroom cloud, and reports of black rain in the area soon afterwards, reminded many people of the atomic bombs dropped on Japan to end the Second World War. There was the evidence of the still-standing trees at the centre, and unconfirmed reports of mutated animals around Tunguska. But the blast of 1908 was more than 1000 times more powerful than the Hiroshima bomb – so where could it have come from? No country on Earth knew how to make any such device at that time.

Some witnesses, it had been asserted, talked of the column of fire changing direction as it plummeted to the ground. That might mean that it was piloted – a space-ship! For hundreds of kilometres around the site the trees and soil contained tiny fragments of magnetite and silicon, and exotic elements such as ytterbium, which could only have come from the blast. Were they bits of a spacecraft? And look what's near by: Lake Baikal, the largest body of fresh water in the world, a perfect place for the safe landing of a doomed starship. The scientists laughed long and hard at that one.

What seems most likely is that it was the rare example of a comet entering Earth's atmosphere and blowing up before it hit the ground. It came in low and in the same position in the sky as the Sun, which may explain why no astronomers spotted it. At the time, scientists have worked out, the comet Encke was crossing our planet's orbit; it seems reasonable to assume that it was a fragment from Encke.

At this distance, once again, it all happened too long ago for anyone to be certain. And OK, so a comet is not as exciting as a stricken starcruiser. But just think: if that piece of comet had stayed up for another hour, it could have been over a crowded city like London or Paris. Now that would have been a real catastrophe.

FILE STATUS
Probably a comet.

Close Encounters of the Third Kind

One can't think of a Close Encounter of the Third Kind without seeing that great glowing mothership hovering over Devil's Peak, or hear a trombone playing that five-note 'Pom-pa-pom-pee-pah!' In fact, many ufologists are rather annoyed with Steven Spielberg's film, for although it was a great piece of entertainment it did mean that everyone now knew what a UFO and its alien pilots were meant to look like. For years after the film was released, sightings were full of glowing orbs and spindly extra-terrestrials. You might wonder whether people were influenced by the film, their minds making leaps to explain the strange by falling back on something they were familiar with.

Of course, not all CE3Ks follow such a pattern.

Casebook: George Adamski

Among the first alleged *contactees* (someone who has met an alien) was George Adamski. He was, he alleged, a philosopher, though he worked in a burger bar in Mount Palomar, California, USA. In 1953 he published a famous book called *Flying Saucers Have Landed*, in which he claimed to be the first person on Earth to meet a visitor from a flying saucer.

In it, he recounted how he and six friends had driven out into the Mojave Desert, hoping to see a UFO. After some searching, Adamski said, he spotted an enormous, cigar-shaped, silvery ship hovering overhead. It telepathically instructed him to follow a dirt road; he did so, then sent his companions back to the main road to watch as he approached where the craft was hovering between two mountain peaks.

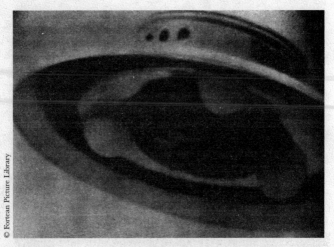

Underside of the UFO allegedly photographed by George Adamski at Palomar Gardens, California, 1952. Yeah, right.

A handsome alien appeared, beckoning to him from a ravine 400 metres away. This being, communicating telepathically and with sign language, said he and his fellows had come from Venus. Their spacecraft were powered by magnetism, and some had crashed on Earth after being shot down. Adamski wasn't allowed to photograph the alien or to enter his ship. Eventually it left, leaving Adamski to write up the tale.

The book was a sensation, and it helped popularize ufology across America. Adamski took to the road, delivering talks on his gentle space friends and showing photographs he claimed he had taken. In effect, he helped to start the trend for conventions and gatherings of ufologists and fans of space creatures.

In his next book, *Inside the Space Ships*, George Adamski went on to claim that he was receiving messages from his Venusian friend, Orthon. He said he had been on many fantastic adventures with the Venusians, flying in their craft to Mars, Jupiter and Saturn. Most amazingly, he claimed to have seen the dark side of the Moon and had witnessed the many rivers and lakes there! As we now know, that far side is nothing more than a deserted, crater-scarred lump of rock. Adamski could only be lying.

It later emerged that Adamski had first written *Flying Saucers Have Landed* as a work of fiction, and he only rewrote it as a true story when it didn't sell. He spoke of 'the flying saucer business', and it certainly made him plenty of money. Some of the witnesses to his first encounter later retracted their story. Perhaps George Adamski did see something initially, but he certainly blew it out of all proportion when he tried to keep the gravy train rolling.

Interestingly, however, even today many of his photographs are presented as genuine, and a small band of followers meet every year at Palomar to celebrate their hero, who died in 1965.

FILE STATUS
Hoax

Don't take me to your leader

Once George Adamski had publicized the possibility of meeting beautiful people from beyond the stars, it seemed as if they were landing all over the place, bringing with them all sorts of heartening messages of galactic friendliness. They were more like characters from a comic book or a cheesy B-movie than sophisticated, civilized beings, but for a time people believed they were real.

Early in 1950, Daniel Fry allegedly approached a saucer that had landed in the desert close to White Sands Missile Base, New Mexico. He spoke to an extra-terrestrial called A-lan, who was in a mothership 1500 kilometres up in space, and was allowed to ride around in the alien's remote-controlled saucer. Fry was instructed to publicize the aliens' message that 'understanding is the key to peace and happiness'. Fry, like Adamski, produced many photos and films of alleged UFOs for another decade. (One wonders whether he also met A-lan's friends, maybe C-live and N-orman.) Others, among them Truman Bethereum and Howard Menger, made similar claims, though – oddly – their aliens all came from different planets.

As time went on, the Cold War paranoia of the 1950s and early 1960s served to turn mankind's view of aliens into one of suspicion and, eventually, of fear. Reports of close encounters increased, but now they were with cold and aloof beings who treated their witnesses with disdain and scorn. More cases in which people had been affected or injured by UFOs were publicized in books like *Flying Saucers Are Hostile* and *Flying Saucers – Serious Business* (which warned against touching or even standing directly under a UFO!). In October 1963, six saucers allegedly attacked a farmhouse in Argentina. A year later, a hunter in California was left hanging in a tree by two robots which emerged from a saucer and attacked him.

As time went by, abductions (CE4Ks) became more common than mere meetings. As a result, the accounts of CE3Ks became more peculiar, almost as if people were trying to compete with the more 'glamorous', and certainly more newsworthy, abduction claimants. The sinister Men in Black came to prominence (see page 64), and Billy Meier began claiming that the UFOs in his photographs had taken him on journeys through time. Some ufologists began to wonder if the aliens were teasing us, playing games for their own amusement – as if the Earth was an intergalactic theme park playing host to holidaying extra-terrestrials!

As the rumours concerning the crashed saucer and alien bodies found at Roswell in 1947 were revived in the late 1970s, stories began to increase about visitors and their saucers being captured. However, because many of these stories came from still-serving military personnel who needed to remain anonymous, the rumours raged unchecked and unable to be proven. 'Crash/retrieval' cases became fairly regular occurrences, though even now they rarely involve civilians.

One strange encounter with a civilian involved 77-year-old Alfred Burton. As he told it, he had settled down with his dog for a spot of night fishing by the Basingstoke Canal, in Aldershot. At around 1 a.m. he was just about to have a cup of tea when a brilliant light descended. It landed on the towpath some way away, and a little while later two short humanoids in green uniforms, their faces covered by visors, approached Alfred. They gestured for him to follow them and led him to their craft. There, they asked his age in 'faltering English' and made him stand under a device that shone with an amber light. After a few minutes one of the aliens said, 'You can go. You are too old and infirm for our purpose.' The old codger returned to his fishing rod, to find that his tea had gone cold; the UFO sped up into the air. Perhaps back on their home planet even now the aliens are telling tall tales about the fisherman they threw back.

Animal Mysteries

Warning: there are some gruesome details in this section.

Some of the nastiest side-effects of the UFO phenomenon have been the injuries done to animals, and in particular to cows, for which the blame has been pointed at aliens. In September 1967, the discovery of the skinned body of Snippy, a pony belonging to a rancher in Alamosa County, Colorado, was certainly horrible enough. Moreover there were 15 circular impressions, like exhaust marks, around Snippy's blood-drained body. A UFO flap was occurring in the area at that time, and in the next few weeks four cows and the same number of horses died similarly grisly deaths. There were more deaths in Pennsylvania that autumn, and since then several hundred incidents have been reported across a large part of the middle of the United States, from Montana down to Texas, and occasionally in other parts of the world too.

The injuries always seem to follow a similar pattern: there are wounds on the body, always clean and surgically precise; various internal bits are missing; and the creature's blood has been drained. Ugh! As well as UFOs, such cases can be accompanied by reports of sinister black helicopters flying around the area. These have led to theories of chemical leaks or secret biological experiments having to be cleaned up by the military. Some farmers are so convinced of the existence of the black helicopters that they have started shooting at any helicopter which crosses their land. Others talk of evil satanic cults making sacrifices and, of course, of obscure experiments conducted by sinister aliens.

In 1987 the FBI launched an inquiry which a year later declared that it was all down to animal predators like coyotes. But animals don't drain out every last drop of blood, even from the capillary veins. And which animal's teeth are so sharp that it can cut between individual cells, as has apparently been demonstrated? Whatever the explanation, outbreaks continue to the present day, though not in the same numbers as ten years ago. In Puerto Rico, meanwhile, the Goat Sucker has started feeding (see page 106).

FILE STATUS
Unexplained

Casebook: Paul Bennewitz

This topic leads directly to a most disturbing case which proves, if nothing more, that the US Government are playing sinister tricks on UFO enthusiasts. It started with the case of Myra Hansen, from Cimarron, New Mexico, in 1980. She had witnessed something strange one night and lost four hours. Under hypnosis, she talked of seeing aliens leave a spacecraft and injure a cow. She shouted at them but was captured and taken away to a UFO. After a rough medical examination, she was shown other UFOs in an enormous underground base before she was returned home.

Dr Paul Bennewitz witnessed her hypnosis as a representative of the Aerial Phenomena Research Organization. Curious about the implications that US scientists were involved in the underground base Hansen had mentioned, and matching that to reports about UFO activity near Kirtland Air Force Base (AFB) at Albuquerque, he decided to monitor the airbase for clues. He managed to film various secret craft that he thought might explain UFO sightings, and he rigged up listening equipment which picked up what he thought could be communications with the aliens.

He'd picked up something all right: secret military communications experiments, and the base knew about it. The Air Force Office of Special Investigations (AFOSI) tried to warn him off. When that failed, they started to feed the doctor a mass of misleading information about aliens, abductions, underground bases and so on. Bennewitz became obsessed with the material and repeated so many of the bizarre claims passed on to him that he was utterly discredited in ufology circles. This incredible behaviour by the military exposes the extraordinary lengths they'll go to in order to guard their secrets – including inventing a double-bluff UFO cover-story. The question has to be asked: how many other UFO incidents are nothing more than a government smokescreen?

> **FILE STATUS**
> Cimarron incident remains unexplained.
> Government fake UFO operation.

Men in Black

Among the strangest contacts with alleged aliens have been with the sinister Men in Black (MiB). These puzzling beings turn up after a sighting or contact and try to dissuade witnesses from continuing with their allegations. What's really odd about these apparently bogus officials is that many of them seem so 'out of time'. They dress in dark suits and ties, and drive old-fashioned but immaculate cars. Of course, there have been many MiBs who did not fit that pattern, but there does seem to be a trend for such sinister agents to arrive, sometimes before a sighting has even been reported, in order to silence a witness – and in every single case the department they say they work for has never heard of them!

For example, in August 1965 Rex Heflin took a series of Polaroids of a daytime disc near a Marine Corps airfield in California. He made copies – which was lucky, because the next day two men claiming they were from NORAD (North American Air Defence Command) turned up and took away the originals – never to be seen again. Two years later, as scientists from Colorado

University were studying his photos, a new pair claiming to be from the Air Force arrived. They asked all sorts of weird questions about the Bermuda Triangle, then left in an odd car. This time he managed to write down their credentials and look at their apparently genuine ID cards – but again the military had no knowledge of such men!

Possibly the most famous case is that of Dr Herbert Hopkins, who helped UFO investigators in Maine, USA, in September 1976, by using hypnosis on a witness. Afterwards, a man dressed like an undertaker turned up at his house wanting to discuss the case. The newcomer's natural reactions seemed subdued or controlled. When he took off his hat, he had a totally bald head, and when he wiped his mouth lipstick was smeared across his face! Eventually the visitor's speech became slurred; he made a remark about a 'loss of energy' and departed, leaving Dr Hopkins none the wiser. A few days later, his daughter-in-law Maureen and her husband were visited by an equally odd couple, a man and a woman. They behaved very strangely, asking the most personal questions, and they walked with very short steps. As they were leaving, the man became paralysed. The woman asked for help in moving him, then he came to life and the pair marched out of the house as if nothing had happened. It was almost as if they were robots, or alien creatures trying to act human.

There have been a number of other cases, in Britain, Sweden, Italy and Mexico, as well as in the USA. In some of them, prominent ufologists have been warned off from investigating UFOs under threat of violence – and in a few instances this has worked. Studies have revealed that, while a few MiB reports involve visits from sinister men, many more are simple phone calls ordering the investigators or witnesses to drop the case.

So who are these Men in Black? Are they really aliens attempting to disguise themselves as humans, trying to keep people away from their secrets? One would have thought that the odd behaviour witnessed in MiBs would attract even more attention. Investigators are a nosy bunch: if someone tells them to drop the case, that could mean they are on to Something Big! Are the MiBs government agents, out to suppress reports of UFO sightings for whatever reason? That argument carries some weight, particularly now it's known that the CIA and FBI continued to collect secret UFO reports long after the alleged closure of Project Blue Book (see page 95). Could they be deliberately acting in an absurd way to destroy the credibility of any ufologist who reports their activities? The answer is unknown.

Ah well, there is no doubt, at least, who the Man in Black who threatened ufologists in Swindon in 1982 was,

Albert K. Bender's sketch of one of the three 'Men in Black' who visited his Connecticut home in September 1953.

because they rigged up a camera and captured him on film. He was a rival ufologist trying to keep them away from a prize case!

We are sure that the Men in Black won't stop you from investigating sightings. They appear to be very few and far between and, despite the threats, there is no evidence that anything bad has ever happened to anyone who's persisted in telling their story. If you do see someone peculiar, dressed in black from head to toe and walking oddly, don't let them scare you. They're just Goths, and they should be shunned as you would any other out-of-date fashion victim.

FILE STATUS
Unexplained

Casebook: Roswell

The most infamous name in modern UFO lore belongs to an unassuming American Air Force Base in New Mexico, and an unassuming time in American history, the late 1940s. In fact, the incident at Roswell took place only two weeks after Kenneth Arnold had reported his silver discs, but it has come to dominate all of modern ufology.

The debris

'The many rumors regarding the flying disks became a reality yesterday when the intelligence officer of the 509th Bomb Group of the Eighth Air Force, Roswell Army Air Field, was fortunate enough to gain possession of a disk through the co-operation

of one of the local ranchers and the sheriff's office of Chaves County.'

That was part of the text of a military press release issued
by the airbase at Roswell, a town in New Mexico, USA,
on 8 July 1947. The base was already famous as the
launch site for the B-29s which had dropped the atomic
bombs on Japan two years previously, but this was just as
big a story. The same day, the *Roswell Daily Record* carried
the headline: '**RAAF CAPTURES FLYING SAUCER ON
RANCH IN ROSWELL REGION**'. This story was sent
out by telegraph to all corners of the United States and
beyond, and soon calls were flooding in from around the
world.

Unfortunately, the sensation did not last long. Six hundred kilometres to the east, at Eighth Air Force head-
quarters in Fort Worth, Texas, General Roger Ramey
called a press conference. It turned out that the whole
affair was a mistake: the crashed debris found at Roswell
was from a secret weather balloon and its radar reflector
– and definitely not from any flying saucer. The press
release had been a hasty conclusion without access to all
the facts and was a mistake. There were no flying saucers.
The story was knocked on the head there and then, and
it slipped away as quickly as it had appeared – until the
1970s, that is, when UFO researchers picked up persistent
rumours that the US military had recovered a saucer, and
maybe its alien occupants too!

The debris from the alleged crashed spaceship had
come from a ranch near Corona, 120 kilometres from
Roswell. Its foreman, Mac Brazel, had turned up at the
office of his local sheriff, George Wilcox, on 3 July, carrying some pieces of an unusual material he had found scat-
tered all over his land. The previous night there had been
a heavy thunderstorm. Right at its heart, there had been
an enormous crash, and the next morning the odd stuff
was all over the place. Something peculiar had fallen from
the sky and broken up on impact.

The sheriff was out of his depth, so he contacted the
authorities at Roswell Air Force Base. The next day,

Major Jesse Marcel, the base's intelligence officer, and another officer arrived at the ranch. There they discovered the unusual debris spread in a wide fan shape for more than 100 metres in both directions. It was strange stuff: although it looked like foil, it couldn't be burnt, it resisted the blows of a heavy sledgehammer and, when crumpled up, it quickly returned to its original shape. There were also pieces of small, I-section beams, embossed with purple hieroglyphics – like you might get on a box of fireworks, one person said. The officers gathered up as much as would fit into their vehicles, and then returned to Roswell for further analysis.

During the next few days it emerged that several other people in the area had seen a strange object in the sky that night, among them two ranchers near Roswell itself. When the press release was put out by the Army, it seemed to confirm everyone's suspicions: a flying saucer had landed in Texas.

The cover-up

The military changed its mind soon afterwards, appearing to demonstrate that nothing more harmless than a weather balloon had crashed, and that was that. When UFO researchers started their fresh examination of the events of that week in 1947, however, they found a whole heap of troubling and contradictory evidence. Firstly, there was that press release talking about a captured flying disc. Was it for real? Had an over-zealous officer inadvertently blabbed a secret that the whole world was waiting to hear?

The press conference called by General Ramey also turned out to be far stranger than everyone had at first thought. Various officers, including Jesse Marcel, had posed for photographs with shredded pieces of aluminium foil. However, these were not from the debris which had crashed at Corona. It turned out that General Ramey hadn't even seen the real fragments when he called the press conference. There was a cover-up, plain and simple.

That was just the start. In 1978, the Roswell researchers began to hear rumours that there had been not one but *two* crashes that night in the Roswell region. The second was an escape pod, perhaps from the Corona spacecraft; it had come to rest either just north of the air base or 220 kilometres west of it, out beyond the first crash site, depending on who you believed. The saucer was almost intact – and four or five aliens had been recovered, one possibly alive! These aliens were all small and hairless, with large heads, and each was wearing a one-piece grey suit. They were taken to Roswell, then shipped off to another base, possibly Wright Field at Dayton, Ohio. Witnesses to the whole affair had been warned to keep quiet under pain of death; but 30 years later many felt they had to reveal the truth. Among them was Roswell's undertaker, Glen Dennis, who had allegedly received a call from the airfield's mortuary officer asking for three child-sized coffins.

So what really happened at Roswell? That's what people have wanted to know for decades, including a US senator who called for an official inquiry. Ahead of that, the US Air Force investigated the affair and issued their own report in September 1994: and, of course, it found no evidence whatsoever of any spacecraft or alien bodies. It was scorned by ufologists, but by then anything which didn't confirm that there had been a crash and that aliens were recovered would have had the same reaction. Roswell had become too big to be swept under the carpet; the case had taken on a life of its own. When the official inquiry came out, in July 1995, it said much the same as the USAF report, but it added that most of the records from the time had been destroyed, without the proper authority, and this meant that any attempt to get at the truth was doomed to failure. Which was mightily suspicious.

The reports haven't stopped some dedicated ufologists from crying 'Cover-up!' The trouble is, it all happened half a lifetime ago. Most of the major witnesses are now dead; the only really important one remaining is Mac Brazel's son, and he was only seven at the time. After five decades memories have grown hazy, and the case has been raked over so much, no one can be sure where real memories end and false ones begin. There have been books and an American TV movie: no one connected with the case could not know all about what was meant to have happened.

In September 1994, the US Government confessed that there *had* been a cover-up at Roswell, albeit a small one. They admitted that the debris shown at the press conference was not that recovered from Mac Brazel's ranch. Their reason for this, however, was that the pieces were from a top-secret Project Mogul balloon, not a saucer. This was a scheme to send high-altitude airships over the Soviet Union to spy on Russian atomic weapons tests. Flight No. 4 had gone astray and had crashed, but the military did not want the devices publicized.

That explanation has been picked over thoroughly by ufologists, but the truth of it cannot be determined. Other theories have also been aired. There has been much talk of Japanese *fu-go* balloons, devices packed with bombs and sent off to fly across the Pacific in the last months of the Second World War. They were made of very tough paper, silvered at the top to avoid overheating the gas inside. That would certainly account for any explosion and any strange hieroglyphic markings, and the Army would never want to admit that the world's only active atomic bomb squadron had been threatened by a two-year-old Japanese bomb! Other theories have mentioned the secret Moby Dick programme instituted by the US Navy and the CIA, in which Skyhook balloons (them again!) were to be sent to spy on Russia. It was also found that on 3 July an experimental balloon made of a new substance, polythene, had been launched from the nearby White Sands Missile Range.

It's certain that something *did* come down at Roswell. It's also certain that the USAF pretended it was something else. But it was all so long ago, and the case has been raked over so much, that the real truth is lost among all the claims and counter-claims.

That video

And then, at the beginning of 1995, ufologists began to hear rumours of an extraordinary film. Taken at the time, it was said to show the wreckage from the Corona spaceship – and the bodies of the aliens found near Roswell! It had been made at the time as a record of the events, and a copy had been kept by the military cameraman who had shot it, one Jack Barnett.

The rumours were, in part, true. The film had allegedly been turned up by Ray Santilli, a businessman who had been searching for rare clips of Elvis Presley. The story went that he had bought 14 cans of film for £100,000. There had been dramatizations about what could have happened at Roswell before, most notably the movie *Roswell*, which starred Kyle MacLachlan as Major Marcel. But this appeared to be the real thing!

When the film was shown to ufologists, it split the community. Some were convinced it was real. The shaky, silent, black-and-white footage of two alien bodies being examined, and the shots of various pieces of debris marked with hieroglyphics was the evidence they'd been waiting for. It was too good to have been faked, they said; it was genuine.

Others, though, were much less convinced. A trio of wartime military cameramen viewed it and declared it to be a fake; none of them would have made a film that was so amateurish, and no stills cameraman had been present, as there should have been. And they had never heard of a Jack Barnett. Others pointed out the presence of plastic bags in the film that were not in use in 1947. A telephone in one shot had a curly lead that made everyone question it, but that, at least, turned out to be accurate. Most importantly, everyone wanted experts to test the actual film stock. As the film's promoters failed again and again to provide any pieces for testing, ufologists began to suspect what everyone else had been saying: the film was a fake, and it would never be tested.

Rarely has so little footage been studied by so many people so intently, and yet many are still undecided about its genuineness. There seem to be too many inconsistencies in it. Indeed, its very existence seems too good to be true. If it is a fake, who made it? Was it put together to make money, or by some enthusiastic amateurs to hoax the UFO community? Or was it more government disinformation, released to make the whole affair's UFO links seem silly, or to draw attention away from the official report's lost and missing evidence? The jury is still out on this one.

FILE STATUS
Probable secret balloon test; awaiting more information. The video is almost certainly a hoax.

Know Your Alien

If you are lucky enough to have something strange crash in *your* back garden during a particularly violent thunderstorm, how will you know what sort of aliens were piloting it? Luckily, there is a handy classification system.

The *Greys* are the most common 'modern' aliens. That is, before such aliens were publicized by books like Whitley Strieber's *Communion*, very few people reported seeing them. Nowadays they seem to be everywhere. They are smaller than humans, maybe 1.2 metres tall, and they are thin, almost spindly. Their skins are grey in colour, and they usually wear one-piece body suits of the same shade – hence their name. They have large heads, with enormous, slanted, almond-shaped eyes, dark in colour, but these may just be artificial covers like a kind of intergalactic sunglasses. They have small noses or none at all, and a very tiny mouth, which implies that the telepathy they are known to use has replaced normal speech. As with all aliens encountered by witnesses, they can speak and telepathically communicate in perfect English and all other languages, which is remarkably clever of them.

The other main type are the *Nordics*. These tend to be encountered in Europe, though in the early days Americans also used to meet them. They are tall, beautiful humanoids, very much like us, with flowing blond hair and handsome features. It is said they are the enemies of the Greys, who are evil; the Nordics just want to help mankind, which is nice. However, Travis Walton reported that both types were present on the craft which abducted him in 1975 (see page 78); perhaps they have formed an alliance to ensnare all mankind under their cruel dominion, ha ha haah! Or perhaps not.

Hybrids are increasingly being reported by abductees. These are half-Grey, half-human, and they are said to be the product of all those nasty medical experiments which the aliens have been carrying out on everybody. They share the features of both sorts but have strangely angelic faces, it is reported, and very wispy, white-blond hair. If you know anyone with hair like that, ask them if they are a space alien's baby and see what they say.

Creatures known as *Neonates* are less common. These are wrinkled, like little Greys, and to look at they resemble an unborn baby. It's possible that they are young Greys, or a subservient species. They share much the same characteristics as that race, including a liking for carrying people off in their flying saucers.

In the 1950s, and particularly after Hollywood started making movies about the flying saucer menace, many people claimed to have seen *Reptilian* aliens, complete with scales and claws. These days they seem to be a bit thin on the ground. Perhaps they went home again.

As well as all those, there are the sinister, human-like *Men in Black*, of course (see page 64). Some aliens have been accompanied by *Robots*, and there is some evidence to suggest that the aforementioned MiBs are also mechanical; it would go some way towards explaining their odd behaviour and jerky movements. Other types have included the small R2D2-style androids which apparently landed in a saucer near a railway track at Quarouble, in France, in 1954.

Non-human monsters are not very common, thankfully. The bizarre creatures seen in Brazil in 1977 by Antonia La Rubia, with their wobbly lizard bodies and robot heads mounted on a single pole like an alien pogo stick, have not been seen anywhere else. It's possible they were only here on a day trip. Giant white maggots like those which crawled across a road at Yssandon, France, in 1960, are very rare.

Men in costumes, though, are far more common. One was captured on film by the Falkville, Alabama, Police Chief, Jeff Greenshaw, in 1973. It looked exactly like someone in a fire-fighting suit with an aerial stuck on his head, but Greenshaw was adamant that he'd photographed it caught in his headlights one night. When he approached it, he said, it ran off faster than his car could travel. Several similar sightings were reported by local residents during the next few days. The trouble was, the photo was found to be a hoax and Greenshaw was asked to resign within the month. What those other people saw isn't known. Perhaps it was space aliens.

Close Encounters of the Fourth Kind

Stories of people actually being abducted by the occupants of spacecraft had a strange beginning. The story of Betty and Barney Hill's alleged experiences in 1961 wasn't told until 1966. A similar case, that of Antonio Villas Boas from 1957, didn't come out into the open until 1969. Since they did, though, they've stayed in the headlines, chiefly because of the role hypnosis has played in discovering hidden memories that may or may not in fact be true. Certainly many dedicated ufologists, even those who believe that there really are alien visitors, argue that hypnosis has been misused in UFO research. Others believe that hypnosis is a vital tool which has revealed a genuine secret history of abductions and sinister experiments by alien beings!

Casebook: Betty and Barney Hill

Among the first abduction stories, and still one of the most argued about, was that of Betty and Barney Hill. They were driving home from holiday on Highway 3 through the White Mountains of New Hampshire, USA, on 16 September 1961. Around midnight, they saw an unusual light in the sky. Barney suggested it could be an aircraft, or perhaps an off-course satellite. It was when it

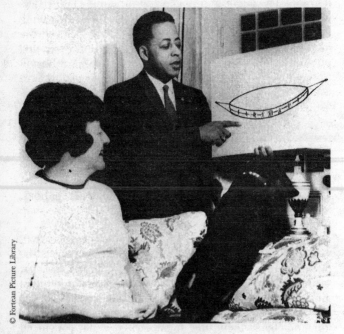

© Fortean Picture Library

Betty and Barney Hill, who believed they had been abducted into a UFO.

changed direction and moved closer, apparently following them, that Betty took out her binoculars. She was shocked to see it was an enormous, pancake-shaped craft with two rows of lighted windows, and it was descending towards them!

Barney pulled off the road, grabbed the binoculars and approached the pulsating craft. Betty heard him repeating, 'I don't believe it! This is ridiculous!' Terrified, the two of them jumped back into the car and raced for home, followed by an unusual beeping noise. When they arrived, they found that the car's paintwork had blotches all over it. Barney's neck ached and his shoes were badly scuffed. There seemed to be some discrepancy in the time, too: it was two hours later than it should have been.

Betty reported the strange sighting to their nearest Air Force base and began to read up on other UFO incidents. Barney's ulcer began acting up. Betty started having intensely disturbing dreams in which aliens blocked the highway, then dragged them into a UFO and examined them. Barney went to see Dr Benjamin Simon, a Boston psychiatrist, and was soon joined by Betty. Four months of hypnosis unravelled the story of what had really happened that night – allegedly.

They had been abducted by small aliens, they said, with grey skin, big heads, large eyes, no nose and slitted mouths. The aliens had taken them to their craft and subjected them both to humiliating medical examinations. Barney remembered being dragged, which would certainly explain his scuffed shoes. After the examinations, the aliens told them many things and showed Betty a map of a star system which she took to be their home.

For his part, Dr Simon the hypnotist believed that, since Betty's story matched that of her nightmares, the hypnotic memory was just an imaginary experience, not reality. It's possible that Barney, whose account differed in tiny details from Betty's, but which matched it in all the big ones, was just echoing his wife's descriptions of her dreams. Back then, the hypnotists weren't convinced that aliens and UFOs were the cause of their patients' problems.

Whatever the truth of the matter, the case caused a sensation when their story was published four years later in John Fuller's book *The Interrupted Journey*. It seemed to be a new chapter in ufology – now the aliens were capturing people and examining them; but hypnosis could reveal the truth. An astronomer, Marjorie Fish, took Betty Hill's sketches of the aliens' star maps and worked out that they were pointing to a star system called Zeta Reticuli. Later, they were matched against a better map by the astronomer Carl Sagan, who discovered 'little similarity' at all. So were they abducted? Their doctor thought not. That night, though, a nearby Air Force radar had tracked an unknown object across the area. Perhaps the Hills did see something unusual and it influenced Betty's dreams to such an extent that she began to believe them. Whatever the truth of the affair, it certainly set the pattern for 25 years of abductions, examinations and hypnosis.

FILE STATUS

Unexplained

Casebook: Travis Walton

There is a very frightening movie about UFOs called *Fire in the Sky*. It's based on the 'true story' of a man called Travis Walton who is abducted by aliens and taken to their vast spaceship, where all manner of scary things happen to him before he is dumped back on Earth, having been gone, not for a few hours, but for five days. Just another work of fiction? You should investigate.

This is what he claimed happened. It was 5 November 1975, a couple of weeks after a film about Betty and Barney Hill had been shown on local TV. Travis, a young lumberjack, and his six mates were returning home after a long day clearing trees in Apache-Sitgreaves National Forest, near Snowflake, Arizona. They saw strange lights shining through the trees. Thinking it might be a crashed plane or some other emergency, the lumberjacks stopped their pick-up truck. Suddenly a gigantic, milky-yellow, diamond-shaped craft appeared above the treetops. Travis Walton jumped out to take a closer look. His friends called to him to come back. Walton stopped behind a log and, hearing his companions and realizing he was being foolish, turned to run back to them.

Everyone else stared in horror as a blue ray blasted from the object, lifted Walton into the air and slammed him to the ground. Thinking he was dead, his friends drove away in panic. When they calmed down and returned, a few minutes later, their friend had gone and there was a distant light in the sky heading away north-eastwards. The police could find no clues, and a search was launched, but to no avail.

Five days later, Travis Walton, scared and shivering, and five kilograms lighter, rang his parents from Heber, 20 kilometres away. He wasn't sure what had happened to him, but his memories returned in violent flashes over the next few days, and hypnosis revealed more.

He had woken up, he said, lying on a table. He drifted in and out of consciousness, thinking he was in hospital. But when he finally came to his senses, he realized that the beings examining him were not human! Around him were several short, big-eyed aliens dressed in dark uniforms. Walton leapt from the table and tried in a panic to escape their clutches. When he failed to calm down, the aliens eventually left the room, and he managed to escape through another door. After exploring for a short while, Walton was joined by a tall, apparently human being wearing a helmet, who led him to a large hangar area with several disc-shaped craft parked in it. Three more humans, each with blond hair and piercing eyes, put something over his mouth and he drifted back into unconsciousness. When Travis Walton woke up again, he was lying by the side of the road and the craft was a rapidly disappearing dot in the sky.

That was his story, but how true is it? It is known that Travis Walton took two polygraph tests, lie detectors in effect. He failed the first and passed the second. He has always stuck to his story, and indeed has now claimed that

© Fortean Picture Library

Alien allegedly seen by Travis Walton after he was abducted near Snowflake, Arizona, on 5 November 1975, drawn from Walton's description by his boss, Michael Rogers.

he has remembered more details which will, when he reveals them, prove the truth behind the whole UFO enigma. To many sceptics this sounds like someone who is inventing more details in order to keep people's interest in his case. There are allegations that the lumberjacks were failing to meet a deadline for clearing the trees and invented the whole thing to get themselves out of trouble. They never did finish that job – but that is understandable if what allegedly happened is true. On the other hand, Travis Walton was well known for his practical jokes, and neighbours were very suspicious that his mother appeared to be unconcerned that her son was missing, abducted by aliens.

Fire in the Sky, incidentally, tells the story from Travis Walton's side but, in typical Hollywood fashion, the makers totally changed most of the details of what happened on the spacecraft so as to make them more dramatic. Oddly, other people have since reported experiencing an abduction very like the one depicted in the film. Could it really be possible that they were making hoax claims, inspired by the film rather than by real events?

FILE STATUS

Possible hoax, but if so a pretty good one. Walton and the others continue to stick by their story.

Aliens can't read

Abductions continued to be reported; when, first, Budd Hopkins's *Missing Time* (1982), then Whitley Strieber's *Communion* (1987) came out, the world at large began to learn about the controversy. And everyone knew about what was meant to happen when you are abducted. The case of Whitley Strieber was a strange and controversial one. He was already a published writer of horror and science-fiction novels; now he was claiming the story of his own abductions was a true story. But was it?

Strieber had been having strange, dream-like memories for years, but one Christmas something happened that made him seek out professional help. On 27 December 1985, in a cabin in New York State, he had woken from a disturbed sleep, feeling very uneasy and with a memory of having seen an owl peering in through the window of his cabin at him in the night. When he sank into depression, he read one of his Christmas presents, a book on abductions, and realized that he had experienced one. Under hypnotic regression, supervised by Dr Donald Klein, he pieced together the supposed events of that night.

He had been awakened by a 'whooshing' noise from downstairs. He wondered if it was intruders. A figure entered his bedroom, and he blacked out. When he woke up, he was being carried through the woods by small figures. Then he found himself inside an untidy domed room, surrounded by small and taller alien figures, who proceeded to conduct a very painful medical examination on him. He remembered seeing his sister, father and various soldiers lying, unconscious, on other tables. Eventually the aliens returned him to his bed. That was startling enough but, as he recounted in *Communion*, his memories went much deeper. He had, he learned, a lifetime of abductions which had started in 1957 when he was 12 and had been taken from a train.

The success of his book brought many accusations from ufologists. It was too good to be true that an author of fiction was coming out with such stuff (particularly as it was selling so well, undoubtedly). Dr Klein thought Strieber might have problems with his temporal lobe that were causing him to hallucinate, but tests seemed to disprove this theory. However, when his second book, *Transformation*, came out, events seemed to have got out of hand. In that volume he talked about being shown around craft full of alien bodies, of levitating and having out-of-body experiences, of hearing voices, and more besides. These days Whitley Strieber does not insist upon the truth of what he once claimed happened to him, but speaks of the alien abduction experience as being a symbol for the uncertain age in which we all live. Yikes.

FILE STATUS

Unexplained, but possibly not an abduction.

Your typical abductee

Since *Communion* and the other books that followed in its wake, the wave of abduction claims has reach near epidemic proportions in the USA. Elsewhere, the 'craze' has not taken off, but abductions have been reported by citizens of many Westernized countries. As the basic medical examination plot has become commonplace, more and more bizarre experiences have been related. It's almost as if witnesses have had to invent something even more horrible than the last person just to get heard. There have been alien babies – first one, then several, then dozens. There have been implants, tiny alien-made devices which have allegedly shown up on X-rays, only to disappear the day after. Who knows what will be claimed next!

Many, many theories have been put forward to explain the abduction experience. The *temporal lobe problems* suggested by Whitley Strieber's hypnotist may provide one answer. Basically, they mean that the different sides of the brain get confused, causing hallucinations and sleepwalking. Even without such a medical condition being present, many people experience very realistic *lucid dreams*, in which the things dreamt appear to be true, and the dreamer believes he or she really is awake and taking part in events.

Sleep paralysis is a perfectly harmless occurrence that many people experience. In fact, it happens every night, but by then you're usually fast asleep. During dreaming sleep our muscles become rigid so that we don't act out our dreams. However, sometimes this doesn't happen properly: it comes on while we are still awake or it stays on when we wake up. It can feel as if one is being held down on the bed; and it has given rise to all sorts of legends as to its cause, including medieval stories of 'night hags'. There are many cases in which a harmless case of sleep paralysis has convinced a UFO fanatic that they are being abducted!

The biggest problem with so many abductions is that of the hypnosis which is controversially used to prise out buried memories afterwards. If it's so easy for a stage hypnotist to persuade twits to pretend they're chickens and make fools of themselves, think how simple it would be for someone who already believed that they'd been kidnapped by aliens to discover it was 'true'. Think how much you already know about UFOs. If you had had a series of strange dreams, wouldn't the suspicion that aliens were the cause cross your mind, even if you knew it's not true? Ultimately, it may prove that the abduction experience is little more than wishful thinking, a fantasy that the believer wants to come true so strongly that it does.

Casebook: Linda Cortile and . . . Perez de Cuellar?

The famous abduction researcher, Budd Hopkins, announced the case of New Yorker Linda Cortile (aka 'Linda Napolitano') as 'the case of the century'; it certainly took abductions to a new level. Hopkins had been regressing Linda for some months and revealing her memories of being abducted by Greys for some years. On 30 November 1989, she turned up for a session saying she had been taken at 3 a.m. that morning! She had been lying next to her sleeping husband when she felt a paralysing numbness creep up her body. Three or four aliens entered the room, and she floated with them through the closed window of her twelfth-floor apartment! She was taken up to a spaceship, where she was medically examined, before being returned to her bed.

Fifteen months later, in February 1991, Hopkins received a letter from two policemen. They had been sitting in a car and they witnessed a woman floating out of her window and into a UFO, which then dived into the East River, by the Brooklyn Bridge. They pin-pointed Linda's apartment and described her accurately. The most amazing thing, though, was that they were bodyguards taking a prominent VIP to the New York heliport; he had also witnessed the whole thing. Indeed, they wondered whether the whole event had been staged for his benefit. Budd Hopkins has never revealed who this VIP was, but the rumour is that he was the then Secretary General of the United Nations, Perez de Cuellar!

This story has been hotly debated, and the facts are very contradictory. The NY heliport denies there were any flights that night, and de Cuellar was (his office says) at home in bed in another country. Linda's numbness sounds very like sleep paralysis. The fact that Hopkins has met only one of the four witnesses, Linda herself, seems highly suspicious. Perhaps he is being fed facts, as Dr Bennewitz was. This case has some way to go yet, but it seems too good to be true.

FILE STATUS

Unexplained, but some very suspicious aspects.

In Case of Alien Abduction

So, Sparky, you woke up this morning and felt a bit weird, did you? Well, think back carefully. In the night, did you have any dreams which seemed particularly real? Dreams about flying out through a closed window, floating through the air in a beam of light? Dreams in which little grey people with big eyes poked you in the tummy then went tut-tut and asked you to cough? Don't trouble yourself; if you can remember it all, you haven't been abducted – you've just been reading too many books about UFOs, you twit. Get outside and play some sport or something.

If the unthinkable happens, though, and you wake up in the middle of the night, lying on a table and surrounded by aliens in what you can only describe as, well, a spaceship, here's what you need to do.

Above all, remain calm. Observe and remember as much as you can. If the aliens seem to be sympathetic, make small sketches or get them to pose for photographs. Have a look around; feel free to open drawers and look in cupboards. Some recently described spaceships can be a bit messy and they let down the popular 'gleaming lights and polished surfaces' reputation aliens have, so don't make sarky comments along the lines of 'Just look at the state of this place!'

If the aliens seem chatty, ask questions. Many of them seem only too happy to natter on about where they've come from, how their spaceships work, and so on. Of course, it's possible that you'll have to learn how to communicate telepathically, but that shouldn't be any harder than learning Norwegian in, ooh, about three minutes. And the effort could be well worth it. You never know: they might even be able to help you with your homework. And what if they are time-travellers – if they can give you a list of the numbers due to come up in next week's Lottery draw, it would prove more than compensation for that embarrassing medical examination!

If you do get talking to some aliens, do us a favour, will you? Ask them the question that's always bothered us: why have they never realized that people would be more likely to notice them if they landed outside the White House or on the centre spot at Wembley Stadium on Cup Final day? Surely aliens, allegedly the possessors of an intelligence far superior to ours, can't be interested in the limited conversations the dorks who see UFOs indulge in. Oh goodness, perhaps that's it: aliens are anorak-wearing nerds too, and they've just popped down to swap fascinating tales of standing in Crewe station with a flask and a little notebook. If this turns out to be the case, our sympathies are with you. Grit your teeth and pretend to be fascinated by everything they say; your horrific ordeal will be over sooner than you think.

Try to grab something and bring it back with you as evidence of your experience. Don't make it too obvious, though. Even the dopiest Grey might notice if you try to joyride out of the mothership's docking area in his prized Sports Model saucer. Go for something small but utterly alien in manufacture, like a Twiglet or a new, previously unknown type of biro.

Have faith, courage and a sense of humour, and use your intelligence. All right, on second thoughts, just do the best you can. It will soon be over and you'll wake up, back in your own bed again. Then you will be able to lie back, relax, and start planning the opening chapter of your book . . . and how you'll spend all the money.

Close Encounters of the Fifth Kind?

If the rumours surrounding the infamous Roswell incident are true, the US military has a captured flying saucer. If all the other rumours about 'crash/retrievals' of alien craft are true, they have a veritable fleet of the things. OK, OK, we're already wobbling on the very edge of credulity with this, so let's take one step further. If they have spacecraft, they're going to be trying to find out all about them. They'll have been taking them apart to see how they work; after all, anything that small which can cross the vast wastes of space must have a pretty cool engine. Maybe they've worked out how they are built, and have constructed some of their own. Who knows – perhaps they've even managed to persuade some daredevil stunt pilots to give the things test flights, and it's these that people are seeing in the sky. In other words, they really are seeing alien flying saucers; it's just that the people flying them are test pilots, not little grey chaps from Zeta Reticuli.

Black secret technology

There is no question that the US military have flown flying saucers. These weren't from the stars, though; they were built right here on Earth and have been test-flown quite openly. The idea that a round, saucer-shaped craft could be the ultimate flying machine was first tested by the Nazis close to the end of the Second World War. The rapid speed of technological discovery brought about by the war had already resulted in the V-1 and V-2 rockets in Germany, and in jet aircraft on both sides. Beyond these, though, were many far more experimental designs. When the Allies captured the secret Nazi research base at Peenemünde, they discovered plans and possible prototypes for flying discs, flying frames, flying wings, and many more. As the years have gone by, of course, a few fanatical ufologists have raked through such discoveries and, using the tiniest shreds of evidence, have decided that such saucers were built and were flown. What's more, they say, the Americans captured them and flew them too, then used them as the basis for their own craft. Then they go and spoil it all by suggesting that perhaps they are all based on captured alien saucers, and can fly using anti-gravity, can travel through time, and all that nonsense. Oh dear.

It's certainly true that the American scientists of the 1950s developed some peculiar aeroplanes. The Chance-Vought 'Flying Flapjack' looked like a huge, round hovercraft. It could fly at up to 640 kph or as slow as 55 kph, and it took off nearly vertically. The trouble was that, when it did so, the lack of any real wings or a tail to keep it stable made it very unsafe indeed, and the plans for it were scrapped. Or were they? Those wily ufologists talk of its secret successor, the XF-5-U-I (snappy name, guys!) that was larger, over 30 metres in diameter, which had solved its stability problems using a row of jet nozzles around its rim. Hey – that means when it was flying it was both saucer-shaped and had a line of lights around its middle. Could it be . . .?

It's certainly true that experiments with the aerodynamic shapes of wings led to experimental craft which were almost all wing. In the USA, the Flying Wing flew quite successfully, though stability was again a problem. But in the late 1950s such designs were put on the back burner, at least until the B-2 Stealth bomber came along.

Secret experimental projects are known as *black projects*; they are kept hidden from prying eyes and have their own, undefined section of the American defence budget. Of the 1994 American defence budget of $84.1 billion, a whopping $14.3 billion was for black projects. Many of the craft built by them eventually enter service, but for every one that does there must be a hundred that don't. But all these bizarre devices have to be tested, even flown in secret. As a result, for years witnesses have been seeing craft which look like aeroplanes but which the military have denied owning.

In the late 1950s, at the height of the Cold War with the Soviet Union, the Lockheed U-2 was the first

American craft to enter service in complete secrecy. In other words, here was this long-nosed, fast, high-flying aircraft which no one knew about but kept spotting, and which the government denied owning! Eventually sightings grew so frequent that the military had to own up; but even then they said it was just gathering weather information high in the stratosphere. It wasn't until one plane, flown by Gary Powers, crashed inside the Soviet Union and caused a dramatic diplomatic incident that the full truth came out. (If you were wondering, the Irish band are indeed named after the U-2 aircraft; bet you thought it was a type of submarine.)

After the crash, the U-2 was replaced in 1964 by the SR-71 Blackbird, another spy plane which had been flying secretly – and quite likely causing more UFO flaps – for several years. This stayed in service until 1990, when it was stood down because satellites could do the job far more efficiently.

Stealth: fighter, bomber and . . . Aurora

However, that doesn't mean this was the end of secret aircraft. Far from it. Since the mid-1960s, the USA had been working on craft which could be invisible to radar. These 'Stealth' craft could, in theory, sneak in over enemy lines without being spotted, thus avoiding defences like enemy planes and anti-aircraft missiles. So, the Americans were testing an invisible plane that could fool radar; the craft were so secret the authorities could never admit that they had them, even to the rest of the armed forces. Sounds like a recipe for a whole wave of UFO sightings!

And this is pretty much what appears to have happened, though the military have never admitted that their craft were the cause. In California in 1975, a mobile radar unit from the US Air Force picked up a strange target flying at around 700 kph. On the next sweep of the radar, it had gone, having apparently flown out of range. But that would have meant it had accelerated suddenly and near-instantly to a speed of more than 3000 kph. Perhaps, in fact, it had merely turned on its stealth cloak.

The sighting was logged as Unidentified; yet again, it seemed that the right hand didn't know what the left was secretly testing.

Strange craft continued to be spotted. In October 1978, film was taken of a peculiar, triangular craft which flew in near silence over Leicestershire, England. (Strong rumours later said that Stealth fighters were being flown secretly at RAF Alconbury, in Leicestershire.) Manta ray-shaped UFO sightings became far more common, and eventually two bizarre new aeroplanes were revealed to the world. The F-117A 'Nighthawk' Stealth fighter and B-2A 'Spirit' Stealth bomber are now familiar shapes following footage of them flying over Iraq during the Gulf War, their peculiar profiles setting new trends in aircraft design.

Even before the Stealths came into active service, there were strong rumours about a newer type of Stealth craft. It was to be a spy plane, a replacement for the ageing Blackbird; unlike the F-117A, it could fly very fast indeed while retaining its radar-invisible advantage. Ufologists and aircraft enthusiasts regularly scan US Government budgets in the hope of spotting something new, and this time they hit pay dirt: in 1985, a black budget report made mention of a multi-million-dollar programme known only as 'Aurora'.

So what does it look like, and what is it capable of? Analysis of unexplained UFO sightings seems to reveal the answer. It is fast, that's certain. In 1991–2, a series of sonic booms every Thursday morning at 7 a.m. were tracked across the San Gabriel Valley in southern California – generated by an unknown aircraft flying at between Mach 3 and Mach 4 (that is, up to four times the speed of sound). Peculiar vapour trails like 'doughnuts on a rope' have been reported near Beale Air Force Base in California. The talk was of a liquid-fuelled rocket engine which pulsed, causing such an individual trail. A sharply pointed triangular aircraft was seen from a North Sea oil-rig platform in 1989, and a sinister, black, triangular craft caused a major flap over Belgium and southern England later the same year (see page 117). Extremely fast-moving radar signals coupled with more bobbly vapour trails have been sighted near the joint RAF–NATO base at Machrihanish in Scotland. This secret base has the longest runway in Europe and has long played host to Blackbirds and, more recently, Stealth fighters.

It seems certain that some sort of new craft was being tested over the USA and Europe. It may be the Aurora, and it may well be a spy plane. Once again the fevered imaginations of the ufologists have been working over-time: the familiar topic of an anti-gravity engine, devel-oped from a similar device in a captured flying saucer, has been mentioned by a few crackpots. It seems unlikely, to say the least. However, don't expect to find out just yet, for it seems that the tests haven't been going so well. In 1995, three Blackbirds were brought back into service due to 'cutbacks and cancellations' in the replacement project.

FILE STATUS

Facts withheld by US Government; await further revelations.

Bob Lazar in Dreamland

In 1988, after the unveiling of the B-2A Stealth bomber, some of the Californian scientists who had worked on it apparently leaked a statement saying that the craft had 'anti-gravity'. So OK, let's indulge the lunatic fringe for a moment. If the B-2 has an anti-gravity engine and, say, the Aurora is powered by a new rocket design copied from a flying saucer, how has this happened? There have been rumours of captured alien craft circulating since the mid-1950s, but it was the revived interest in the aftermath of Roswell that really got the ball rolling. In 1972 rumours abounded about a secret programme called Project Snowbird. It said that the government was *back engineering* from a captured saucer or twelve; that is, they were taking them apart and copying what they found.

Where is this happening? One possible location is Area 51, the top, nay toppest, secret research base at Groom Lake in Nevada, USA (see page 114). Known as

Dreamland, it is a vast complex of hangars, bunkers, factories, test areas and the longest runway in the world – and officially it does not exist. So there! Stealth aircraft were developed and tested there, as was the ill-fated Strategic Defence Initiative ('Star Wars') programme. No wonder curiosity and speculation run riot!

'We don't have UFOs out there. What goes on out there is classified,' said Air Force spokesperson Major Mary Feltault in an interview in May 1995, responding to claims that the base was home to all manner of extraterrestrial devices. But try telling that to Bob Lazar.

In 1989 he appeared on an American TV news show, claiming that he had worked at Area 51. His area was S-4, the most secret part of the whole base, and his position had a security clearance 38 levels higher than the Top Secret 'Q' clearance he used to have while working on SDI projects at Los Alamos. His job, he said, was back engineering an engine from a captured and all-too-real alien flying saucer.

It was called Project Galileo, and it was housed in nine hangars built deep into the side of the mountains. The craft he had been allowed to inspect was around 10–12 metres in diameter and 5 metres high, made of dully polished aluminium. Inside, it had seats that were too small for an adult human. This craft, he said, was jokingly known as the 'sports model', and it was in such good working order that it had been test flown. It had an anti-gravity engine which he had examined at length, his advisers communicating directly with a number of tiny, spindly-legged figures who stayed back in the shadows! As to how the engine worked, he was able to offer all kinds of complicated explanations which are near-incomprehensible to anyone without three degrees in experimental atomic physics. Of course, they are also completely uncheckable.

What *was* checkable was Lazar's employment record. The military denied he had ever worked for the government, but then they won't even admit that the enormous Groom Lake facility exists. Some sectors of the UFO community have taken his claims to heart and have allegedly turned up much more convincing evidence. Others have looked at Bob Lazar's past and have discovered that some of his claimed academic qualifications fail to check out. Some even say that if the military wanted someone to spread disinformation, perhaps in order to confuse ufologists and keep them from revealing very real defence secrets, Bob Lazar would be an excellent choice.

FILE STATUS

It's mind-blowing, but it's probably a hoax.

The Real UFO Investigators

In the TV show, *The X-Files*, Mulder and Scully work for the US Government's Federal Bureau of Investigation, the FBI. In reality – to many people's intense disappointment! – there isn't really an X Files Department. Sorry.

Or at least, it's not known by that name . . .

Department A2

In the United Kingdom, all unusual sightings which occur in British airspace are handled by the Ministry of Defence, more specifically by Secretariat Air Staff, Department 2A – better known as 'The UFO Desk'! Their brief is to assess every sighting for its potential threat to the security of Britain. They are not there to prove or disprove that UFOs exist, though they are happy enough to confirm that a sighting is 'Unexplained'. How they manage to decide that an object is unknown while offering no threat to security has not been explained. However, when we rang them up, we were told that the official view was as follows: 'To date, the MoD is not aware of any evidence which substantiates the existence of extraterrestrial craft or life-forms.'

The Civil Aviation Authority, which handles commercial airliners, also has investigators, who work for the Independent Joint Air Miss Working Group. This was set up to handle air traffic near-misses, but at times it can include incidents when aircraft get buzzed by strange lights or unknown objects, as in the case of a British Airways passenger jet which was buzzed by a huge, triangular-shaped craft when coming into Manchester Airport on 6 January 1995. The intruder had passed so close to the BA aircraft that one of the two pilots ducked involuntarily, and both officers clearly saw the vehicle. The report stated that the matter 'remains unresolved', but added, 'to speculate about extraterrestrial activity is not within the Group's remit'.

Top Secret: Access Denied

Elsewhere in Europe, the Belgian SOBEPS department has had a lot on its plate following the flying triangles sighted in their airspace (see page 117). The French have GEPAN, which started as a very open-minded and helpful department liaising with ufologists, but which is now very secretive. A suggestion to expand its operation to cover all of the European Community was turned down by MEPs in February 1994. Most other Westernized countries have an official military department which tries to explain unusual sightings in their airspace.

It is in the USA that the greatest amount of investigation goes on – which is not surprising since it is the world's hotbed for UFO sightings and abduction reports. Officially, the matter is now all centralized at the UFO Reporting Centre, part of the US Coast and Geodetic Survey, in Rockville, Maryland. However, it has long been known that the FBI, the CIA and the super-secret National Security Agency all continue to keep files on UFO incidents.

Over the decades since Kenneth Arnold's momentous

sighting, various investigations have been initiated in the USA in response to waves of sightings. All of them have reached much the same conclusion: that there are no aliens; but some UFO sightings remain unexplained – and each one has been used to play down the UFO phenomenon, with the result that ufologists have had to keep yelling 'Cover-up!' at every stage.

Project Sign (1948–9) was a US Air Force investigation. Its results were inconclusive. It was transformed into *Project Grudge* (1949–52); its final report covered 244 cases in over 600 pages. Of these, 56 defied easy explanation, and the conclusion, while denying an alien source, did at least admit that life on other planets was a possibility.

In January 1953 (though kept secret for years), the CIA's *Robertson Panel* sat and deliberated for three days on the subject of UFOs. They studied 75 cases and decided that, while there was no proof of anything weird, the 'continued emphasis on the reporting of these phenomena does result in a threat'. The panel's only suggestions were for an elaborate disinformation campaign and for the surveillance of independent UFO research groups.

The biggie was *Project Blue Book* (1952–69), which collected every sighting it could lay its hands on, as well as photographs and films, many of which have never been released. When it ended, it had more than 25,000 sightings in its files. These were eventually examined by a committee led Dr Edward Condon, who unfortunately stated before even beginning work that his inclination was to tell the government to 'get out of the UFO business' because it was all frauds and mis-sightings. And a leaked memo revealed that 'the trick would be, I think, to describe the project so that to the public, it would appear a totally objective study'; in other words, it was to be anything but.

The *Condon Report* (1969) was 1485 pages long and studied 87 of the Blue Book's best sightings. Strangely, Condon's introduction (all that was read by many, especially journalists) said that there was no proof of aliens and 'further extensive study of UFOs probably cannot be justified'. Those who read a little further found that, in direct contradiction to this statement, a quarter of the cases were listed as 'unsolved'! Strange. The Condon Report persuaded the US Government to close down Project Blue Book – or, at least, apparently so.

Thanks to the 1976 Freedom of Information Act, many secret documents have now been made available for ufologists to study. These haven't always been useful: one released by the NSA had a two-line title that was totally crossed out save for the word 'UFO', and its entire readable text ran thus: 'In this document the author discusses . . .' with the rest of it censored. Not very helpful.

CENTRAL INTELLIGENCE AGENCY

WASHINGTON 25, D. C.

OFFICE OF THE DIRECTOR

MEMORANDUM TO: Director, Psychological Strategy Board

SUBJECT: Flying Saucers

1. I am today transmitting to the National Security Council a proposal (TAB A) in which it is concluded that the problems connected with unidentified flying objects appear to have implications for psychological warfare as well as for intelligence and operations.

2. The background for this view is presented in some detail in TAB B.

3. I suggest that we discuss at an early board meeting the possible offensive or defensive utilization of these phenomena for psychological warfare purposes.

Walter B. Smith
Director

Enclosure

However, some nuggets did appear. One file revealed that, in the 1950s, the CIA planned to get Walt Disney to make silly UFO cartoons to stop the public taking the idea of aliens seriously! More importantly, another memo revealed that only the public pretence of investigating

UFOs was to be stopped in 1969; all serious reports would continue to be investigated at the uppermost level of security. No wonder ufologists continue to think there is a cover-up!

Casebook: The Majestic Report

This appeared to be confirmed by the astonishing case of the MJ.12 documents, also known as the Majestic Report. It is a series of top-secret documents that, if true, show just how deeply the government's cover-up went. However, that's a very big 'if'.

In December 1984, an American TV producer was sent an anonymous package containing photocopies of two documents. One was a memo from September 1947, signed by President Truman; the other, nine pages addressed to President Eisenhower and dated November 1952, was a briefing for the President about a hidden council of scientists and politicians who apparently reported directly to the US President on matters relating to UFOs, and in particular the recovered spacecraft and aliens captured at Roswell! Wow!

All the men on the list existed and all held very credible senior positions. But they had all died by 1984, so they couldn't be asked if it was all true. Then someone started to apply some logic: researchers found that the signature by President Truman on the first memo was genuinely his – because it was identical to one on an ordinary memo. Since no one ever signs his or her name exactly the same way twice, it had to have been copied off that other memo. And if the Truman memo was a fake, the Eisenhower documents which referred back to it must be too. A forensics expert specializing in typewriters found that the machine which typed the Truman memo wasn't made until 1963. The TV producer declared he'd found a high-ranking officer who could authenticate the report – who turned out to be a USAF sergeant with a conviction for falsifying documents. Let's face it: they were fakes!

That didn't stop the conspiracy theorists, though.

Some said that just because the Majestic papers were false, that didn't mean the committee didn't exist! Oh, brother! Since then, more documents have appeared, claiming to be handbooks and further briefings from the MJ.12. They're very cleverly written, for all the rumours and allegations, from Roswell and Area 51 to Zeta Reticuli and anti-gravity engines, are woven into their text. But they are all expanding on a fake, so how can they be true? Whatever the truth of it, the MJ.12 documents are now on the Internet (see page 128); pop along and have a good laugh at your leisure.

```
FILE STATUS
Hoax hoax hoax!
```

Independent researchers

With all these officially sponsored government cover-ups, conspiracies and general mucking around with the Real Truth going on, it's no wonder that there are so many civilian UFO investigation groups out there. The first were started in the USA in the early 1950s, but just about every country which experiences UFO sightings has one or more. In the USA, the prominent Centre for UFO Studies (CUFOS) was founded in 1973 by the late J. Allen Hynek, who had been a Project Blue Book adviser but who had grown fed-up with the dismissal of unexplained sightings. The Centre holds computer files on 80,000 sightings. It has a core of 26 full-time scientists, who are assisted by investigators from the other main US group, the Mutual UFO Network (MUFON).

In the UK, the British UFO Research Association (BUFORA) are the largest organization. They have over 1000 members, with around 50 active investigators. The police and the Ministry of Defence pass unusual cases on to them from time to time; if you ever have to report a sighting, you may be put in contact with one of their people. Addresses for all these groups, and those in other countries, are on page 126.

Is Anything Out There?

When they were busy debunking all the thousands of UFO sightings they had collected over the years, the various US Government reports into the phenomenon were very forthright that sightings were not due to any visiting aliens – while at the same time reaffirming a belief that there were aliens out there. Because, for all the logical explanations for those strange lights and shapes in the sky – whether Venus, secret spy planes, ice crystals or bits of grit in the witness's eye – there continue to be sightings which cannot be explained. So the question must be asked: if there really are vehicles of some sort, where are they coming from?

Dimension hoppers

At the moment, time travel is still only a theory, a complicated spin-off from the Theory of Relativity and all that brain-aching stuff. Perhaps in the future our descendants will have discovered how to harness it, and it is they who are popping back to take a peek at us. Perhaps abductions are merely their way of testing us for pollution and diseases; perhaps they think we can cope better with a flying saucer than with a time machine. And is the government working with them in exchange for some smart advanced technological know-how? If so, you'd think they'd do something more useful with it than build another pointy spy plane.

Or perhaps they come from another dimension (presumably a different one from all those Yetis). Using strange machines, perhaps they have ripped the fabric of reality and crossed over into our world. Such theories have certainly ripped the fabric of the 'not very likely'.

Creatures beyond our understanding

For several years after seeing those silver discs over Mount Rainier, Kenneth Arnold continued to report sightings. On one occasion he was convinced he'd seen a strange, transparent creature floating high in the sky near his aeroplane. Astronomer Carl Sagan has suggested that gaseous creatures could live high in Jupiter or Saturn's atmosphere; could they also dwell in our own? To do so, they would have to be very light indeed, perhaps like gas-filled jellyfish. Theoretically they are possible, and they certainly might explain some of the odd falls of squidgy stuff that splatter the ground occasionally – but they hardly explain close encounters or abductions.

Ghosts and spectres have been seen by mankind for centuries. Now experts are wondering whether modern man is interpreting unusual sightings in a different way. In medieval times a strange shape was claimed to be an angel or a religious manifestation; later, it was a ghost or spirit; perhaps now they have become spacemen. What they really are, though, continues to be obscure. It's a nice theory, but it would be nicer to have some proof.

Inner and outer space

When they weren't being totally evil and murderous, the Nazis were very fond of absolutely barmy ideas about witchcraft and the Holy Grail – and especially the theory of the Hollow Earth. This says that inside our world there is another one, with the entrances at the poles. Down there are refugees from Atlantis, or possibly creatures called Deros who want to enslave our world, using scary flying saucers. Believe it or not, such theories continued to be popularized by a few crackpots into the 1950s and beyond. Ho hum.

The most likely explanation for any non-human visitors has to be that they have come from another planet out in space. But just how possible is this? At the turn of the century people talked of there being life on Venus, Mars and beyond. Slowly but surely, astronauts and remote probes have sent back information suggesting that each planet in turn is too barren or too poisonous to sustain life. So now mankind is looking further afield.

Man has been scanning the stars for decades in search of life. Since the 1940s, television and radar signals have been leaking into space; more recently, simple codes have been broadcast at likely-looking stars. Our space probes are sent off carrying greeting plaques showing where to find us. In turn, we scan the radio waves and peer at pictures of constellations to see if anyone else out there is doing the same. Various Search for Extraterrestrial Intelligence (SETI) programmes have continued to probe into the likeliest corners of our galaxy.

At the end of 1995, scientists analysing data from the enormous new Hubble space telescope announced amazing news: they had found evidence of not one but *three* planets circling distant stars! The stars were wobbling slightly in their orbits, indicating that something else near by was affecting their gravitational pull. It is likely that these stars – 51 Pegasi, 70 Virginis and 47 Ursae Majoris – are just the first of many that will prove to have planets.

The trouble is, though, that everything is much too far away. Those three stars are between 35 and 42 light-years away; in other words, if you could get a starship that travelled at the speed of light, it would still take 35 years to reach the nearest one! The very nearest star to our own Sun is Proxima Centauri, a 'mere' 6 light-years away. Zeta Reticuli, where Betty and Barney Hill's mysterious abductors allegedly came from, is more than 20 light-years distant!

Those figures, of course, are assuming that one had a vehicle travelling at the speed of light. The physics behind it all would make your brain hurt, but basically it's impossible (sorry, *Star Trek* fans, but 'warp speed' just isn't on). Even if you could get a vehicle up to one-fifth of the speed of light, say, the amount of fuel you would need would be positively enormous – and then you would need the same amount to slow you down again when you finally arrived at the other end, 100 years later!

And that's assuming you knew where you were going. The new planets found by the Hubble telescope are being checked out, because it is so easy to make mistakes amidst all the complicated mathematics. In July 1991, astronomers at Jodrell Bank announced that, contrary to all the theories, they had discovered evidence of a planet circling a distant pulsar. The trouble is, a pulsar is a star that's exploded – any planet near by would have been consumed in the explosion. It turned out that they had forgotten to account for the fact that the Earth too was moving: in effect they'd discovered themselves!

And if you think that's daft . . . spare a 'Duh!' for Project Phoenix in California. One of their scientists thought he was listening to radio pulses from space, relayed from a massive telescope in Australia. He kept picking up a distinctive pattern of radio signals at the same time every evening. For ages he studied them, trying to work out what they were. Eventually it came to him: he was picking up the microwave ovens in the canteen downstairs. Ping!

Wormholes

And the same to you. So it's accepted that space is so vast that travelling even to somewhere like Proxima Centauri would be a greater undertaking than anything ever done before by the human race. So now the physicists, astronomers and mathematicians are going back over all that relativity stuff again, looking for loopholes. Or, rather, *wormholes*. The science-fiction ideas of hyperspace and jump drives have been taken seriously, and the boffins are trying to see if they could be true. The theory is that space/time isn't a big, open area, it's curved. One part of the galaxy twists around and joins on to another; if we knew where this happened, perhaps we could take a short-cut. And another thing: if light is affected by the pull of gravity, that means it can go round corners. Which means that theoretically if you looked hard enough you could see the back of your own head. We'll stop there, because *our* heads are hurting. If you can handle more and you're an ultra-boff, try *A Brief History of Time* by Stephen Hawking.

Is there life on Mars?

OK, so it's all but impossible for an alien race to keep popping over for a quick fly-by in their saucers before nipping back home in time for tea. But what about a star-travelling race that actually flew about in a giant craft which supported them for generations, in effect a steerable planet? Is there any evidence that they might have visited us, if only once?

Funny you should ask. In 1976, after several months' travel, the Viking I space probe finally slipped into an orbit 1800 kilometres above the surface of the planet Mars and began sending back pictures. Thousands of them. Over the years, these have been painstakingly studied and have provided masses of new data about our neighbouring planet. Two photographs, however, revealed some very controversial things indeed.

Both are looking down on the region of Mars called Cydonia, and it doesn't take long to see what all the fuss is about. Plum in the centre, there is a tiny shape: it looks like a face . . . a face on the surface of Mars! When this was spotted, the area of both photos was computer-enhanced to provide more detail, and the 'face' was picked out in all its strange glory. It was about 500 metres high, and over a kilometre long, and it appeared to be made of rock. Near by, the enhancement had picked out another feature, a distinctly artificially made, five-sided pyramid!

NASA, somewhat understandably perhaps, played down the apparent discovery. The images were created by shadows, they said, and were merely an optical illusion, just as people see a man in the Moon, or shapes in clouds. The trouble is, the two photographs they were working with had been taken from quite different angles, and the face and pyramid were there in both of them! A three-dimensional computer model was made, and it produced an astonishing image of a slightly eroded pyramid standing near a human face gouged out of a rocky outcrop and staring straight out into space.

Now it's time to play 'sceptics and believers' again.

Some people look at the pictures and see a face and a pyramid; but these are only illusions, caused by the tendency of the human mind to see a face whenever two eye-like blobs are next to each other, particularly if they're inside a face-like circle. Others have looked closer and have reported finding more details – pupils in the eyes, for example. The similarity to the Egyptian Great Pyramid and the Sphinx is remarkable, they say. People have looked around for other features near by and have claimed to find a six-sided pyramid and other shapes they have called the Fortress, the City, the Tolus, and more. A scientist involved with the case, Richard Hoagland, has gone even further and has found 'evidence' of regular mathematical shapes and straight lines linking the positions of the various features.

But are people simply looking too hard? If there is a face and a pyramid at Cydonia, how did they get there? One theory has it that the face is a deliberate attempt to signal to Earth that we are not alone. An ancient star-faring race came past our planet thousands of years ago, saw that we were still primitive ape-men and departed again. But they left a recognizable version of our face that we would see only when we were close to venturing out into the stars ourselves. The pyramid, meanwhile, was to show that the face wasn't just an accident of nature.

Of course, by this stage you may, quite understandably, just want to put your fingers in your ears and yell, 'Shut up! Shut up!' As with so much of ufology, a great splurge of detail has been spun out of a very tiny fragment of information. The next mission to Mars will be the Observer space probe, which is intended to create a map of the whole surface. Perhaps that will reveal the truth.

FILE STATUS

Unexplained but probably wishful thinking.
New pictures may provide more answers.

Left Behind?

There may not be life on the Red Planet, but it may surprise you to learn that there are pieces of both Mars and the Moon here on Earth! Scientists have found tiny clusters of minerals in combinations that are found only on those other planets. It has been suggested that they were blasted off by the impacts of meteors and that they ended up being pulled by the Earth's gravitational field until the fragments themselves fell as meteorites.

That's just the start of it. For decades some scientists have been working on proving the theory that comets and meteors have been acting like giant bumble-bees, innocently carrying things around the galaxy and depositing them on different planets. Some diseases sweep our world in cycles similar to that of the 76-year interval between sightings of Halley's Comet. Other diseases spring out of nowhere; could the likes of Legionnaire's Disease and the Black Death have been delivered here by a comet? Maybe the very building blocks of life were originally carried to our planet by such an interstellar wanderer, adding the final atoms to what was already present, and causing life to start to evolve. It's still wildly theoretical, but it's not totally implausible.

Then consider the Venus fly-trap, that carnivorous plant with leaves like hands that close around insects. It grows naturally in only one spot on Earth, an area about 150 kilometres around Wilmington, North Carolina, USA. It's the only member of a species which is found nowhere else. It thrives after a forest fire; it likes heat and ash. The area where it grows wild appears to be a series of craters from a meteor shower. Just as you may have done, a few scientists have put all those pieces together and have suggested that maybe, just maybe, the Venus fly-trap plant is not native to our planet. Perhaps, just perhaps, it's actually from (whisper it) outer space. Of course, if this had been proved you might have heard about it already. It's still a theory, nothing more, but it does open up the whole subject of strange and out-of-place creatures, some of which don't appear to belong on our planet.

Casebook: The Jersey Devil and the Goat Sucker

In the state of New Jersey in the USA, tales of a strange creature called the Jersey Devil or the Leeds Devil go back as far as 1790, and come as near as this year. It has been sighted by various witnesses, but its description varies somewhat. It's been seen as a very tall, faceless, hairy creature; a 'ram-headed weirdie', a walking 'flying lion'! One night in December 1993, a park ranger was driving on a narrow and lonely road through Wharton State Forest. In the shadows on one side of his headlights he saw a large dark figure emerge from the woods. He screeched to a halt as it crossed the road in front of him. It was upright, well over 2 metres tall, and its black fur appeared matted and slicked as if it was wet. It didn't seem to have any forelegs. Just before it strode away into the night, it turned and stared at the ranger with burning red eyes! It seems the Jersey Devil still haunts the woods.

Fantastical creatures have been reported in many isolated areas and with such regularity that some might wonder whether there really was something to all the cases. The Australian bunyip, for example, appears to have forgotten it was just an Aboriginal folk-tale, and keeps frightening solitary hunters and cattle drovers. It may be a cousin of the Yowie, a huge, 4-metre-tall hairy creature from Western Australia. In the lakes of British Columbia, Canada, scaly reptile men like extras from *The Creature from the Black Lagoon* have been spotted; perhaps they in turn are related to the spooky Lizard Man of South Carolina.

But the current favourite for top monster is Chupacabras, the Goat Sucker of Puerto Rico! The island nation was in the grip of a wave of UFO sightings in December 1994 when something started killing goats, sheep and cows by sucking every last drop of fluid from them through three small, round wounds. More than

2000 cases have been reported since then and, while the authorities claim that the attacks are all from stray dogs, baboons or some wild animal abandoned as a pet, those who have encountered the Goat Sucker have a different explanation.

Chupacabras is said to be like an upright dinosaur or lizard but with no tail. It has an oval head and an elongated jaw with fang-like teeth. Its upper limbs are two small, three-fingered arms; its legs are strong and thick and they end in three toes on each foot. Strong, coarse hair sprouts from its body, but eye-witness reports can't seem to make their minds up whether it is dark or light in colour. Most surprisingly, it is said that a membrane stretches from its arms to its sides, allowing it to fly! Who or what it is has yet to be determined, but perhaps the truth will soon be discovered. Strong rumours suggest that two beasts were caught, early in 1996, and were taken away to the USA for study. On the other hand, perhaps all we are witnessing is an exaggerated flap caused by a few wild animal attacks. Time will tell.

FILE STATUS

As yet unexplained; watch out for breaking news.

Cryptozoology

It's a long word and it means the study of 'hidden animals', that is, creatures which science does not know about or does not accept as existing. Everyone thought that an odd-looking fish called a Coelacanth died out 70 million years ago, because its fossils were not found in rock younger than that date. In 1938 a live, 1.5-metre-long specimen was caught off Mauritius and now there are examples in many large aquariums around the world. Our planet, particularly the sea, has not by any means been totally explored. In the last two years alone, new varieties of deer and ox were found in Vietnam, a long-legged puma called an Onza turned up in Mexico – and a tree-kangaroo was discovered in Papua New Guinea.

Such creatures are all relatively small, but one of the most consistent sets of monster sightings continues to be of a man-monster. In Tibet and China it's the Yeti; in Canada people have encountered the Sasquatch; in western USA it's Bigfoot; and there are many more. In all such cases, solitary hunters and explorers have claimed to have encountered them – or at least they have come across inexplicably large trails of footprints. Every so often a new set of photos of such prints comes back from the Himalayas with a mountaineering expedition. Each time, experts suggest that they might only be ox or wolf prints that have expanded in the warm sunshine.

More proof continues to be required before science knows the truth. Pieces of scalp, claws and skins from both Asia and America have proved to belong to normal creatures, most notably bears. The famous colour film of Bigfoot, taken at Bluff Creek, California, in 1967 by Roger Patterson and Bob Gimlin, is astonishing, but it does look awfully like a fat bloke in a gorilla suit. Footprint casts supplied by the pair didn't match the apparent size of the creature in their film. More recently, rumours abound on the Internet of a Bigfoot suit made by a Hollywood special effects man who'd worked on *Planet of the Apes*. Once again, for all the sightings and claims by

Photo Patterson/Gimlin, © 1968 Dahinden

A frame from a movie film of 'Bigfoot' taken by Roger Patterson, 20 October 1967, at Bluff Creek, northern California, USA.

witnesses, it comes down to the fact that there still isn't any real, concrete evidence; where are all the Bigfoot and Yeti bones? On the other hand, that's what they said about the Coelacanth.

Nessie

And if science can accept the Coelacanth, could they eventually work out what it is that appears to be living in Loch Ness?

Legends of something living in the loch have been around for centuries – just as they have around every third body of water in the world. It was when a new road opened on the north side of the loch just after the First World War, though, that there were repeated sightings of a long-necked creature. Sightings continue to the present day – indeed, people now go on monster-hunting holidays to Loch Ness with the express purpose of seeing the beastie – but, despite everyone's efforts, no one has come up with any proof.

One of the problems is that serious study keeps getting hampered by hoaxes. The most famous picture of the monster was the 'surgeon's picture', apparently taken by Dr Robert Wilson, near Invermoriston in April 1934. The curved neck and small head rising up from a larger body became everyone's image of Nessie. Trouble is, what the photograph shows is a model, made from a clockwork submarine and several tins of modellers' plastic wood bought in Woolworths. It seems obvious now, perhaps, but the photograph was accepted as genuine until 1994!

Proof was once again thought to be very near when underwater photos taken by an American researcher, Dr Robert Rines, showed the 'gargoyle-shaped head' and 'upper torso, neck and head' of a monster. They turned out to be the end of a giant plastic Nessie which had sunk in Urquhart Bay during the filming of the 1969 comedy, *The Private Lives of Sherlock Holmes*. Oops.

People still keep seeing things, though, and cameras keep capturing strange ripples moving in the water. On

© Fortean Picture Library

Three shillings from Woolworths. The classic photograph taken in 1934 by London surgeon Dr Robert Wilson.

the other hand, the loch is a strange place anyway. It's long and deep, bleak and rather spooky. Winds blow down the loch, causing freak waves to rise out of nowhere. In the water are floating logs, mats of rotting vegetation, otters, and much more. If you go looking for a monster in conditions like that, you are probably going to see one, whether it's really there or not.

Among all the sightseers and amateur monster-hunters are some more serious scientists studying the lake and its mysterious inhabitant. Among their theories have been suggestions that it might be a colony of fish, such as giant sturgeons, trapped in the loch after the last Ice Age. The theory was put forward that there were caves linking the area to the sea; the trouble is, Loch Ness is 16 metres higher than sea level and shows no sign of going down. One researcher managed to make a surprising film of a red deer swimming across the lake, stills of which look very similar to many snaps of Nessie. Despite that, there remain many inexplicable sightings of something in Loch Ness and, despite all the research, we seem to be no nearer the truth.

What a weird and wonderful world

Nessie isn't the only lake monster in the world by any means. 'She' has many rivals in countries around the globe. There's Champy, from Lake Champlain, Vermont, USA; Nahuelito, from Lake Nahuel Huapi, Argentina; Issey, from Lake Ikeda, Japan; Ogopogo, in Lake

Okanagan, British Columbia, Canada; and the Changbai Queer Animal, from the tongue-twisting Tianchitianchi Lake, China. And that's just for starters, and it covers only fresh water, not the sea. Water covers more than 70 per cent of the Earth's surface, and within its depths many undiscovered monsters may lurk. Giant squid and octopuses were confirmed only this century, and the first giant Megamouth shark was reeled in only in 1984. There have been sightings of strange sea-creatures around most of the world's coastlines, from the Nessie-like Morgawr seen near Falmouth, Cornwall, to sea-serpents which have attacked ships way out in the middle of the ocean.

There is so much we don't know about our planet. Who needs space aliens? If you ask us, this world is more than weird enough already!

World Alien Hot Spots

Fancy seeing some UFOs? You cannot predict these things, worse luck, but go to a *window area*, a place where it seems that many sightings happen, and you may have more of a chance. When you are doing research for your own investigator files, keep a note of where new reports are coming from. If there are more than a handful in one area, you have a *flap* on your hand; if there are more than a dozen over a whole country, it's a *wave*! Over the next few pages we'll cover the most important areas in the USA, the home of UFO sightings, and Great Britain.

Here are more examples of classic encounters from the last 15 years. Even though waves go away, people continue to report sightings over these areas more frequently than elsewhere. As you can see, most of the world's countries have witnessed UFO sightings! Only Africa and the Indian sub-continent have not reported any major waves.

UFO Hot Spots: World

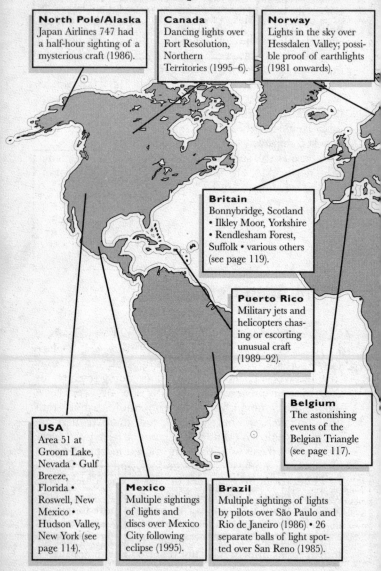

North Pole/Alaska
Japan Airlines 747 had a half-hour sighting of a mysterious craft (1986).

Canada
Dancing lights over Fort Resolution, Northern Territories (1995–6).

Norway
Lights in the sky over Hessdalen Valley; possible proof of earthlights (1981 onwards).

Britain
Bonnybridge, Scotland • Ilkley Moor, Yorkshire • Rendlesham Forest, Suffolk • various others (see page 119).

Puerto Rico
Military jets and helicopters chasing or escorting unusual craft (1989–92).

Belgium
The astonishing events of the Belgian Triangle (see page 117).

USA
Area 51 at Groom Lake, Nevada • Gulf Breeze, Florida • Roswell, New Mexico • Hudson Valley, New York (see page 114).

Mexico
Multiple sightings of lights and discs over Mexico City following eclipse (1995).

Brazil
Multiple sightings of lights by pilots over São Paulo and Rio de Janeiro (1986) • 26 separate balls of light spotted over San Reno (1985).

Finland
Mothership and drones confuse two sailors, off Liska (1981).

Russia
Voronezh: UFO sightings and CE3Ks with tall, silver-suited beings by dozens of schoolchildren (1989) • Perm: Two UFOs and tall, silver-suited occupants seen by a milkmaid (1989) • Samara: Triangular UFO attacks a radar station (1990).

China
After predictions by a wise man, a UFO seen over Ghizhou Province (1980) • A truck driver frightened off a UFO and two aliens by wielding a crowbar (1979).

Israel
Soundless saucer over Haifa; later a possible crash (1985) and various witnessed landings (1987–9).

Zimbabwe
Multiple witnesses see a saucer evade two air force jets over Bulawayo (1985).

Australia
Nullarbor Plain, Western Australia: glowing ball of light that makes your voice squeaky (1988) • Rosedale, Victoria: domed craft emptied enormous watertank and left burnt ring on grass (1980).

New Zealand
Glowing lights repeatedly witnessed and captured on film over North Island (1978–9).

American aliens

The USA all but invented UFO sightings, and some of their hot-spots have fascinating stories. Even when it seems that a series of sightings has been started as a hoax, many more, genuine sightings seem to follow. It's almost as if the UFOs are coming because people are there to see them!

Roswell

There isn't any greater incidence of UFO sightings over Roswell, New Mexico, than anywhere else. People go to Roswell and to Corona, a couple of hours' drive to the west, because that was where it happened: a saucer came down, aliens were captured, the works. The town is practically the unofficial capital of the UFO industry, so it's no wonder people want to visit it. It has two fine museums which have attracted more than 120,000 visitors since 1992 with various exhibits, including models and mock-ups of the important stages in the alleged Roswell incidents of 1947.

If you want to see UFOs, though, you would do better going to Gulf Breeze.

Groom Lake and Area 51

Groom Lake is the enormous dry lake in Nevada, two hours north of Las Vegas, which is home to Area 51, 'the most popular secret air force base in the world', as a local ufologist puts it. This is Dreamland, where Bob Lazar claimed to work on one of nine captured flying saucers. Also known as the Pig Farm, the Box and Paradise Ranch, it has been the birthplace of America's spy planes, from the U-2 to the Stealth, and to Star Wars weapons and satellites. As such, it is a fiercely secretive area; indeed, it is so confidential that it doesn't appear on any maps, and the US Government continues to deny that it even exists. It does, of course – and there are even photographs of it, which have come from Russian spy satellites.

People come to Area 51 to soak up the unusual atmosphere around such a sinister and top-secret base, and just to watch the lights of the test craft buzzing overhead. We mean, who knows what they're flying around up there at night. It could even be one of those saucers! It's certainly been reported that lights have been seen making manoeuvres which seem to be beyond the capabilities of normal craft: stopping dead, hovering, then accelerating to insanely fast speeds.

Catching sight of the base itself is very difficult, as the Pentagon has recently expanded the boundary to include the only real decent viewpoint. Anyone setting foot beyond that boundary is liable to a $600 fine. This is likely to be delivered by the scary 'Cammo Dudes', armed private security men who wear uniforms with no markings and drive white jeeps. As the signs say, they are authorized to use Deadly Force. The best vantage-point is now from Tikaboo Peak with a telescope, if you can stand the one-and-a-half-hour climb.

The nearest town is Rachel, Nevada, a small roadside truck-stop on Highway 375 that has greatly benefited from the wave of paranoid speculation and casual interest in Area 51. Even though it has a population of around 100, it plays host to several thousand interested visitors every year. The town's sole bar, the Little A-Le-Inn, is famous in ufologist circles, and is easily recognizable by its cheery sign that proclaims: 'Earthlings always welcome.'

Early in 1996 the State authorities helped the area's tourism along further by renaming Highway 375 the 'Extraterrestrial Highway'. Four signs declare this fact; they are readable from the road – and by anyone looking down from above.

Hudson Valley

This area, to the north of New York, was plagued by sightings of boomerang- or triangular-shaped craft. The flap was at its highest between 1982 and 1986, but sightings continue to be made – almost 5200 at the last count. A similar boomerang-style craft has been spotted by dozens of witnesses over Williamsport, Pennsylvania, since February 1992.

Gulf Breeze

The very best UFO-spotting site in the world, even more fascinating than Dreamland, is the small resort of Gulf Breeze in Florida. It may prove that the first flap was triggered by a hoaxer, but that hasn't stopped the sightings from continuing. As local ufologist Robert Oechsler points out, 'What is so remarkable about Gulf Breeze is that we are now in the tenth year of constant activity. Sometimes it's a daily activity.'

Strange lights had been reported in the area since the mid-1980s, but only occasionally. The real story begins when a local builder, Ed Walters, claimed to have snapped a whole series of incredible UFO pictures using a Polaroid camera, which he sent to the local newspaper. The *Gulf Breeze Sentinel* was unimpressed at first, but one property of a Polaroid photo is that it can be magnified to bring out details. When this was done, the pictures were incredible. Indeed, they were so crisp and clear that they almost begged a verdict of 'Hoax!'. Unlike the fuzzy blobs or contemporary photos, they all showed a plainly circular craft with its lights and windows visible.

Walters produced more pictures over the course of the next five months. He confessed to an investigator that he had been abducted and a device had been implanted in his brain, so he always knew when a UFO was near. Representatives from MUFON gave him a tamper-proof, stereoscopic camera which he used to take more pictures, but analysis of the film revealed that the UFOs were very small. A simple method of taking a double-exposure Polaroid was demonstrated by experts. A sketch of how to build a model like the one in his pictures was found in Walters's house, but he passed a surprise polygraph test. However, his credibility was ruined, and after his 39th photo he claimed that the implant had vanished as oddly as it had arrived.

Gulf Breeze, however, had by now acquired a reputation as a good place to see and photograph UFOs, and this belief continued – and continues today. Since 1988, people have flocked to the resort with their cameras and camcorders. What's more, they keep on managing to take pictures of UFOs. It's almost as if the presence of the people is making the UFOs appear. More likely, someone is making sure that all those wealthy tourists get the pictures they came for: many witnesses have discovered that their precious UFOs were nothing more than small hot-air balloons warmed over fires and allowed to drift over the bay from Pensacola. It isn't certain who's doing this, but that doesn't seem to stop the UFO fans from coming or the camera shutters from whirring. Gulf Breeze will be the world's favourite skywatching site for years to come.

FILE STATUS

Combination of hoaxes and real sightings.

The Belgian Triangle

UFOs are as numerous over Europe as anywhere, but the Belgian Triangle flap of 1989–91 was something very special. Totally unrelated to the Bermuda Triangle or the Dairylea Cheese Triangle, these events centred around thousands of sightings of an immense triangular aircraft of unknown origin. In fact, the sightings became so numerous that the worried Belgian Air Force began to co-operate with local UFO groups in a frank and open manner; now there's a turn-up for the book.

The sightings began on 29 November 1989 (strangely, the same day that Linda Cortile claimed she was abducted in New York), over the town of Eupen, near the border with Germany. Twelve policemen saw the craft, a dark triangular shape in the sky, picked out with a small light at each tip and a larger one at the centre. It was almost silent, save for a low humming or buzzing noise, and appeared capable of hovering, or at least of travelling at a very slow speed indeed. The UFO was visible for well over an hour before flying off. There were many reports from other witnesses over the next few weeks, all of the same three-sided craft.

Eventually the volume of reports became so numerous that something had to be done. So, on the night of 30/31 March 1990, the Belgian Air Force co-ordinated a nationwide skywatch. The response was incredible: more than 13,500 reports were phoned in and nearly 2,700 written statements, from both members of the military and civilians. There were even some blurry photographs, but nothing conclusive.

At the height of the flap, two NATO radar stations picked up an object within their range. A pair of F-16 fighter interceptors were scrambled from Beauvelain Air Force Base. They managed to close on the object, using their radar, and got a 'lock' on something solid. Every time they did so, however, the craft broke away again. They didn't manage to see it visually. Eventually, after nine attempts and six locks, the triangle dived down towards the ground and was lost among the irregular terrain.

In the aftermath of the reports, the Belgians accused the Americans of testing secret Stealth aircraft over their country. This was flatly denied; all Stealth aircraft are stationed in the USA, was the official line. Off the record, American Air Force personnel told UFO investigators a somewhat different story, though they could not reveal what the craft were or what they were up to. It was confirmed when the French Government learnt that the Americans had secretly photographed one of the French nuclear reprocessing plants using a Stealth aircraft. Sneaky.

It wasn't just Belgium which got buzzed by the sinister flying triangle that night. Across most of southern England, too, there were remarkably similar sightings by civilians and military personnel. Possibly the best was made by an RAF officer at an air force base in Staffordshire. He had heard about the supposed UFO flap on the radio and decided to pop out for a walk and see if he could see anything – only to find an enormous black triangular craft of unknown origin gliding calmly by, 120 metres over his head!

In Belgium the sightings dwindled to a trickle by the end of 1991. In Great Britain, however, they continued to be seen, until the majority of sightings were of triangular UFOs. There was a flap over Lincolnshire involving just such a craft in December 1993 and again in January 1994, and other sightings have come in from all parts of the country.

FILE STATUS
Probably secret spy plane sightings, maybe including some new models.

United UFO Kingdom

The USA may be UFO Central (and Belgium the Triangle Capital of Europe), but Great Britain also has a long history of witnessing strange lights and craft. There were almost 300 sightings reported to the MoD in 1994, and many more were passed on to BUFORA and other independent investigation groups.

The flap over Warminster, Wiltshire, in the 1960s was among the most intense anywhere in the world – at least until Gulf Breeze came along – and sightings can sometimes still be seen in the area today. More recently, in the aftermath of the Belgian Triangle, further reports of similar mysterious craft have come in from around the country; they appear to be particularly common near Glastonbury, in Bournemouth and Lincolnshire.

UFOS: Hot Spots Over Britain

Central Scotland
Long series of unusual sightings from commercial aircraft – mostly glowing lights – are continuing (1995–).

Balmoral, Scotland
Lights chased off by two Harriers; thankfully, Her Majesty not in residence at the time (1995).

Bonnybridge, Scotland
Still-continuing UFO flap (1992–) (see page 123).

Ilkley Moor, Yorks
Former policeman abducted by aliens; later snapped photo of a being (1987). Another UFO sighting and possibly another abduction, rumoured to be of another policeman. Many sightings of UFOs in the area.

Lincolnshire
Many triangular craft seen; note that Lincs is home to many US air bases (1994—).

Stanmore, Middlesex
Multicoloured UFO appears to fire at the ground near RAF Bentley Priory, witnessed by several police officers (1984). More sightings recently.

Rendlesham Forest, Suffolk
Crashed object near an RAF base witnessed by dozens of US airmen (1980) (see page 120); more recently, glowing green lights (1994—).

Chichester, Sussex
Numerous witnesses spotted two dome-shaped objects; same craft reported for several days (1996).

Marlow, Bucks
Three glowing balls captured on video by civilian witness; later witnessed by others (1996).

Todmorden, Lancs
Policeman Alan Godfrey abducted from panda car in famous case (1980); many sightings and abduction reports from the area ever since; centre of a flap.

Warminster, Wilts
Infamous home of the biggest British flap; sightings continue to be made in the area (1964—9).

Glastonbury, Wilts
Long a home to the unexplained, recently home to a wave of sightings of a dark triangular craft (1995—).

Rendlesham Forest

What was it that crashed in Rendlesham Forest, Suffolk, at Christmas 1980? Some areas of the British military seem to have their theories, but they're not telling. In fact the incident only really came to light when the report of the base commander, Lieutenant-Colonel Charles Halt, was released in America via their Freedom of Information Act.

On 27 December 1980, a radar station at RAF Watton tracked an unknown object until it disappeared over Rendlesham Forest. Two hours later, two American gate guards at RAF Woodbridge on the edge of the forest reported a strange light in the trees outside the gates. They went to investigate and discovered a clearing had been smashed in the trees. A metallic, triangular object hovered in the clearing, emitting a dazzling white light. It was 2–3 metres across and 2 metres tall. When the men ventured closer, it moved away into the trees.

The next morning, three depressions were found in the ground, and background radiation in the area had doubled. The following night there was another light in the middle of the trees, this time an intense red 'like the Sun'. As various witnesses, including Lt-Col. Halt, watched, the device broke into five separate white objects, then disappeared. Three star-like objects were then seen in the sky, flying away rapidly.

The official explanation offered by the MoD was that they'd all been confused by nearby Orford Ness lighthouse. Hardly. Most of the witnesses were extremely reliable, and Halt himself had made a tape-recording, reporting events as they actually happened.

So what was it? Suggestions have included a secret experimental craft, possibly being used for mind-control or disorientating enemy troops. Other ideas have included a stray nuclear device and a captured satellite engine; but the truth has not emerged over the years. Rumours that alien beings were seen in the vicinity of the craft, and that Lt-Col. Halt communicated with them using sign language, have threatened to turn the incident into the 'British Roswell', but it would appear that they are all hearsay with no real evidence to back them up.

More recently, as has been the case at locations where a major sighting has occurred, there have been further sightings of lights, and a number of instances in which vehicle engines have been affected.

FILE STATUS
Unexplained

Bonnybridge

The most recent British flap has been over the Scottish town of Bonnybridge, near Falkirk. Starting in 1992, the area has been home to all sorts of strange lights in the sky and flying discs. These have been photographed and videotaped. All in all, there have been more than 2200 separate sightings in the area, with 250 left unexplained, and they are continuing to this day.

It appeared to start when a local man, George Wilson, put a note in the local paper asking if anyone else had had an unusual sighting like the one he had witnessed. Incredibly, hundreds of people replied. It seemed that the area was in the middle of a veritable plague of UFOs: saucers, triangles, cigar-shapes and many glowing balls of light. All the members of a fire crew attending a blaze near Shieldhill had witnessed a small red object, then had been buzzed by a glowing white ball of light. A man returning home late at night was followed by a bright white light; when he reached home, his wife was able to capture it on the family camcorder. The results are doubtful, but there appears to be a cylindrical shape within the light.

In 1994, the additional complication of abduction was added when a young couple delivering a satellite dish late at night both lost two hours after a large black saucer-shape descended on to their car. Under hypnotherapy both have described classic Greys.

The wave shows no sign of going away. Skywatchers, attracted by the apparent ease of making a sighting, have begun arriving. The area is enjoying a tourism boom and, as long as people go on seeing lights, it's likely to continue.

FILE STATUS
Mixture of the unexplained and mis-sightings caused by flap.

The Truth Is Out There

There can be no doubt that most of the strange things people see in the sky can be explained with ease. New theories are being developed all the time to cover most of those (very few) oddities which appear to slip through into the 'Unexplained' category. Many of the more involved encounters and abductions are soon revealed as hoaxes or over-developed wishful thinking. The secret conspiracies between governments and aliens appear to be a mixture of more hoaxing and the natural distrust of ufologists who have been lied to by the authorities in the past.

But the fact is that, for now, there must remain that percentage of cases which have no explanation; it's small, granted, but it's there. Time will tell whether they are as-yet-undiscovered natural phenomena or genuine evidence of extra-terrestrial beings. Something, though, is going on and we don't know what's causing it.

What is needed is proof: solid, undeniable proof. That's why the world needs UFO investigators, good upright people like yourself who can go out there and track down the truth, who won't be fooled by obvious mis-sightings or swayed by paranoid talk about secret conspiracies. Don't fall into the trap of seeing UFOs because you are looking for them; remember that this world has enough weird corners even before you start adding space aliens. Let this book be your guide, and let your most trusted piece of equipment be your brain. Look, just get out there and solve the most pressing mystery of the age, will you?

We know you can do it. Good luck.

Field Support for Investigators

UFO investigators out in the field are loners, trusting no one, examining everything in search of the Real Truth. However, there are a few trustworthy, independent agencies to whom investigators can turn for help with their investigations. You should also do your research. Know your stuff: keep files on all the famous cases, swot up on the classic hoaxes and mis-identifications, get involved. Here are some handy resources that may come in very useful in your continuing investigations.

Organizations

As you can imagine, many of the people who join UFO groups, particularly local ones, are believers. They want every last odd shape in the sky to be a spacecraft, regardless of the facts. However, the larger groups have learnt how to be objective. They will say so when something definitely isn't an alien craft, and they are prepared to admit that some sightings are unconfirmed. If you think you have made a sighting, follow the guidelines on page 40, then report it to BUFORA or to your local group.

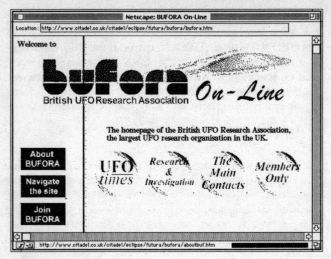

Great Britain

BUFORA (British UFO Research Association):
16 Southway, Burgess Hill, Sussex, RH15 9ST
UFO Magazine: 1st Floor, 66 Boroughgate, Otley,
near Leeds, LS21 1AE

World

ACUFOS (Australian Centre for UFO Studies):
PO Box 728, Lane Cove, New South Wales,
Australia 2066
AESV: BP 324, 13611 Aix-en-Provence, France
AFJ: Box 11027, s – 60011 Norrkoping, Sweden
CENAP: Eisenachenweg 16, D-6800, Mannheim 31,
Germany
CLSV: Corso Vittorio Emmanuelle 108, 10121 Torino,
Italy
CSICOP (Committee for the Scientific Investigation of
Claims of the Paranormal): PO Box 703, Buffalo, NY
14226, USA
CUFORN (Canadian UFO Research Network): Box 15,
Station A, Willowdale, Ontario, M2N 5S7, Canada

CUFOS (J. Allen Hynek Center for UFO Studies): 2457
West Peterson Ave, Chicago, IL 60659, USA
MUFON (Mutual UFO Network Inc.): 103 Oldtowne
Road, Seguin, TX 78155, USA
UFO Research Australia: PO Box 229, Prospect,
South Australia 5082

Further reading

A dedicated investigator will know the subject inside
out. Unfortunately, it has to be said, far too many of the
hundreds of UFO books which clog the shelves are
written by believers, people who are looking and hoping
for spacecraft rather than trying to explain what they
are actually seeing up there. Beware: everyone has an
agenda!

Here are some of the most useful sources, from
both rational writers and some more biased believers,
that you should be able to find or order in your local
library.

Above Top Secret; Beyond Top Secret, *Timothy Good*
The Complete Book of UFOs, *Peter Hough &*
Jenny Randles
The Crop Circle Enigma, *Ralph Noyes*
Encyclopaedia of the Unexplained, *Jenny Randles &*
Peter Hough
On the Track of Unknown Animals,
Bernard Heuvelmans
Open Skies, Closed Minds, *Nick Pope*
The Truth About the UFO Crash at Roswell,
Kevin D. Randle & Donald R. Schmitt
The UFO Encyclopaedia, *John Spencer*
UFOs: a Manual for the Millennium, *Phil Cousineau*
UFOS: the Complete Sightings Catalogue,
Peter Brookesmith (the very best book on the subject
we've found)
UFOs: the Definitive Casebook, *John Spencer*
The Walton Experience, *Travis Walton*

The X-Files Book of the Unexplained
  Volumes 1 & 2, *Jane Goldman* (excellent!)
Fortean Times magazine
UFO Magazine

Further watching

Keep your eyes open for many more TV programmes
and films cashing in on the extraordinary success of *The
X-Files*. Many documentaries tend to be sensationalist or
based on the unchallenged assertions of believers; but
they are a great source of entertainment if nothing else.

The X-Files
Close Encounters of the Third Kind
ET – the Extra-Terrestrial
Fire in the Sky: the Travis Walton Story
Independence Day
Mars Attacks!
Men in Black

Also, various documentary series such as:

Future Fantastic
The Unexplained
Strange But True?
The Real X-Files
Equinox, and many, many more

There are also dozens of video collections, most of
them from the USA, which generally bundle a few minutes' worth of dodgy 'UFO' footage with long rehashes of
the same old stories. Most of them are to be avoided like
the plague; if they were any good they'd have been on TV
long ago.

Further surfing

If you are lucky enough to have access to the Internet,
you'll discover that it's a haven for UFO investigators of

all stripes. The Net's image as a free forum has made it an attractive place for the spreading of the craziest theories. As with all areas of your investigations, the truth is hidden there somewhere – generally amidst a huge swathe of frothing drivel.

World Wide Web

Aliens, Aliens, Aliens: No idea what this one's about.
http://www.xensei.com/users/john9904/

Area 51 FAQ: That's Frequently Asked Questions, about the world's most secret airbase.
http://www.infi.net/~psyspy/area51/re/faq.html

BUFORA On-line: Report sightings or check up on what everyone else is seeing.
http://www.bufora.org.uk/

The Circlemakers: The latest patterns and the wildest theories.
http://www.hrc.wmin.ac.uk/circlemakers/home.htm

Conspiracy Web: Paranoid? You will be after reading
http://www.awpi.com/ConspiracyWeb/index.html

Flying Saucer Review: Quarterly magazine for believers.
http://www.cee.hw.ac.uk/~ceewb/fsr/fsrhome.htm

Fortean Times: The popular magazine of the unusual, on-line at
http://www.forteantimes.com/

ISCNI: That's the Institute for the Study of Contact with Non-human Intelligence.
http://www.iscni.com/

Loch Ness: Och, the monster's on-line the noo.
http://www.lochness.co.uk

Ron Bertino's Alien Information: Sightings, theories, all kinds of mad stuff.
http://www.iinet.net.au/~bertino/alien.html

Roswell Web Site: All the details on the crash, the cover-up and that video.
http://www.roswell.org/ss

Strange Magazine: Including their Top Ten Strangest list which, when we looked, included an Invisible Flying Hippo! http://www.cais.net/strangemag/home.html

The UFO Files: Pictures and articles in a huge archive.
http://linex3.linex.com/ufo/

The Ultimate UFO Page: Links to just about every UFO site on the Net there is.
http://www.serve.com/tufop/

World Wide Times: An immense UFO archive.
http://www.aloha.com/~jet/wwt/

The X-Files: Website devoted to the TV show.
http://www.rutgers.edu/x-files.html

Newsgroups

alt.alien.visitors

alt.conspiracy.area51

alt.paranet.abduct

alt.paranet.forteana

alt.paranet.paranormal

alt.paranet.skeptic

alt.paranet.ufo

alt.paranormal.crop-circles

alt.tv.x-files

alt.ufo.reports

UFO-Speak

Abductee: Someone who believes he or she has been kidnapped by aliens and then returned.

Abduction: Being taken away by aliens up into their spaceship, and then returned.

AFB: Air Force Base.

Alien: A being not of the human race, and probably not from this planet; also space alien.

Back-engineer: To copy advanced alien technology in order to build powerful new human devices, such as military aircraft; also reverse engineer.

Ball lightning: A rarely seen globe of electricity, often used as an explanation for a UFO sighting.

Believer: A person who thinks that there are aliens visiting the Earth, committing abductions, and that there is a government cover-up keeping the facts secret.

BEM: Bug Eyed Monster; avoid at all costs!

Cone of silence: A sudden unnatural stillness that occurs just before many encounters.

Contactee: Somebody who claims to have met an alien.

Debunking: Proving that an alleged alien encounter was a hoax or a mistake; done by a debunker.

Disinformation: Sending out wrong information in order to cover up or mislead.

Earthlight: Strange balls of energy allegedly formed by earthquakes or movements of the Earth's crust.

ET: Extra-Terrestrial, not of this Earth; often used to refer to aliens who are friendlier than most.

Experiencer: Another word for abductee.

Flap: A series of sightings or encounters in one area over a short period of time; also see *wave*.

Flying saucer: A common term for a UFO which appears to be an alien spaceship.

Foo fighter: Strange balls of light that appeared around fighter planes during the Second World War and later.

Fortean: Relating to unusual phenomena, e.g. raining showers of fish; named after their investigator, Charles Fort.

Ghost rocket: The name coined for various meteor-like UFOs sighted over Scandinavia just before and after the Second World War.

Grey: The most common type of humanoid alien encountered: short, with a big head and spindly limbs (also spelt the American way, *gray*).

Hypnotic regression: Sending someone into a trance in the hope that they'll remember something which happened to them; very unreliable.

IFO: Identified Flying Object; what a UFO becomes when someone explains what it really was.

Lenticular cloud: A rare, disc-shaped cloud that looks like a flying saucer.

Ley line: Allegedly a natural line of energy running across the Earth's surface; used to explain why some ancient sites are in lines.

LGM: Little green men; most aliens aren't like that, apparently.

Meteor: A piece of rock which enters the Earth's atmosphere and glows as it burns up.

Meteorite: The solid core of a meteor which falls to Earth.

MiB: Men in Black, sinister men (and sometimes women) who, it is claimed, turn up after sightings and deter people from investigating.

MTE: Missing Time Experience, in which a contactee finds he or she has jumped or lost a few hours.

OOBE: Out-Of-Body Experience; a sense of leaving one's own body and floating up into the air.

Paranormal: Anything that cannot usually be explained by one of the five senses.

Plasma: A section of air that's very highly charged with electricity, causing it to do odd things.

Sighting: Seeing a UFO.

Skywatch: Sitting around watching the sky for UFOs; done by a *skywatcher*.

Sun dogs: Strange weather phenomenon that makes it look as if there are two or more Suns in the sky; also called *mock suns* (more properly, *parhelia*).

UAP: Or Unidentified Atmospheric Phenomenon; a

UFO that is more likely to be a strange weather pattern than a spaceship.

UFO: Unidentified Flying Object, of course, but not all UFOs are spaceships – the term means anything not immediately explained. Also *UAO*, Unidentified Aerial Object.

Ufology: The study of UFOs and aliens; done by a *ufologist*.

UUO: Underwater Unidentified Objects; strange things are found in the sea as well as the sky!

Vehicle interference: When, during an encounter, a car engine stalls or stops dead.

Wave: A large number of sightings that go on for a long time and over a wide area.

Window area: A specific location in which many UFO sightings occur.

Index

You Can Surf the Net

by Marc Gascoigne

Take a trip into cyberspace with this amazing new guide.

Menu: The Internet Explained
Setting Up
Exploring the Electronic
Final Frontier

Help: What is the Worldwide Web?
What's out there?
How do you start?

Search: Reviews of the best Web sites
The weird world of the Web
School links and free software

It's here. It's now. It's the future.

READ MORE IN PUFFIN

For children of all ages, Puffin represents quality and variety – the very best in publishing today around the world.

For complete information about books available from Puffin – and Penguin – and how to order them, contact us at the appropriate address below. Please note that for copyright reasons the selection of books varies from country to country.

On the world wide web: www.penguin.co.uk

In the United Kingdom: Please write to *Dept. EP, Penguin Books Ltd, Bath Road, Harmondsworth, West Drayton, Middlesex UB7 ODA*

In the United States: Please write to *Consumer Sales, Penguin USA, P.O. Box 999, Dept. 17109, Bergenfield, New Jersey 07621-0120*. VISA and MasterCard holders call 1-800-253-6476 to order Penguin titles

In Canada: Please write to *Penguin Books Canada Ltd, 10 Alcorn Avenue, Suite 300, Toronto, Ontario M4V 3B2*

In Australia: Please write to *Penguin Books Australia Ltd, P.O. Box 257, Ringwood, Victoria 3134*

In New Zealand: Please write to *Penguin Books (NZ) Ltd, Private Bag 102902, North Shore Mail Centre, Auckland 10*

In India: Please write to *Penguin Books India Pvt Ltd, 706 Eros Apartments, 56 Nehru Place, New Delhi 110 019*

In the Netherlands: Please write to *Penguin Books Netherlands bv, Postbus 3507, NL-1001 AH Amsterdam*

In Germany: Please write to *Penguin Books Deutschland GmbH, Metzlerstrasse 26, 60594 Frankfurt am Main*

In Spain: Please write to *Penguin Books S. A., Bravo Murillo 19, 1° B, 28015 Madrid*

In Italy: Please write to *Penguin Italia s.r.l., Via Felice Casati 20, I–20124 Milano*

In France: Please write to *Penguin France S. A., 17 rue Lejeune, F–31000 Toulouse*

In Japan: Please write to *Penguin Books Japan, Ishikiribashi Building, 2–5–4, Suido, Bunkyo-ku, Tokyo 112*

In South Africa: Please write to *Longman Penguin Southern Africa (Pty) Ltd, Private Bag X08, Bertsham 2013*